AMERICAN
SOCIAL
MOVEMENTS

THE ANTINUCLEAR MOVEMENT

Jennifer Smith, *Book Editor*

Daniel Leone, *President*

Bonnie Szumski, *Publisher*

Scott Barbour, *Managing Editor*

GREENHAVEN
PRESS ®

THOMSON

GALE

San Diego • Detroit • New York • San Francisco • Cleveland
New Haven, Conn. • Waterville, Maine • London • Munich

LIBRARY OF CONGRESS CATALOGING-IN-PUBLICATION DATA

The antinuclear movement / Jennifer Smith, book editor.
   p. cm. — (American social movements)
Includes bibliographical references and index.
ISBN 0-7377-1152-3 (lib. : alk. paper) — ISBN 0-7377-1151-5 (pbk. : alk. paper)
   1. Nuclear disarmament—History. 2. Antinuclear movement—History. I. Smith, Jennifer, 1970– . II. Series.
JX1974.7 A543 2003
327.1'747—dc21
                                    2002072065

CONTENTS

Antinuclear activism is rooted in religious pacifism. Pacifists developed the tactics of demonstration and resistance that would later be central to the antinuclear movement at its peak.

A military demonstration of the atomic bomb is unnecessary because detonation on a barren island would be adequate warning to the Japanese. The top priority should be an international agreement to regulate the use of atomic energy to prevent a postwar arms race.

Atomic weapons do not discriminate in their destruction. The scientific community must unite and demand that the U.S. government enact a nuclear weapons freeze as a step toward the complete disarmament of world arsenals.

When the atomic bomb was dropped on Hiroshima, those who escaped immediate death had to battle flames that threatened to engulf the city. Survivors who jumped into the safety of the Ota River found themselves surrounded by the dead and dying.

Chapter 2 • THE MOVEMENT AND THE NUCLEAR ARMS RACE

Chapter 3 • THE MOVEMENT TO END NUCLEAR POWER

mission's lack of response and return to business as usual shows that political and economic concerns outweigh the value of human life.

Chapter 4 • THE MOVEMENT TODAY: THE CAUSE REMAINS ACTIVE

Chapter 5 • PERSONAL NARRATIVES AND VOICES OF PROTEST

FOREWORD

Historians Gary T. Marx and Douglas McAdam define a social movement as "organized efforts to promote or resist change in society that rely, at least in part, on noninstitutionalized forms of political action." Examining American social movements broadens and vitalizes the study of history by allowing students to observe the efforts of ordinary individuals and groups to oppose the established values of their era, often in unconventional ways. The civil rights movement of the twentieth century, for example, began as an effort to challenge legalized racial segregation and garner social and political rights for African Americans. Several grassroots organizations—groups of ordinary citizens committed to social activism—came together to organize boycotts, sit-ins, voter registration drives, and demonstrations to counteract racial discrimination. Initially, the movement faced massive opposition from white citizens, who had long been accustomed to the social standards that required the separation of the races in almost all areas of life. But the movement's consistent use of an innovative form of protest—nonviolent direct action—eventually aroused the public conscience, which in turn paved the way for major legislative victories such as the Civil Rights Act of 1964 and the Voting Rights Act of 1965. Examining the civil rights movement reveals how ordinary people can use nonstandard political strategies to change society.

Investigating the style, tactics, personalities, and ideologies of American social movements also encourages students to learn about aspects of history and culture that may receive scant attention in textbooks. As scholar Eric Foner notes, American history "has been constructed not only in congressional debates and political treatises, but also on plantations and picket lines, in parlors and bedrooms. Frederick Douglass, Eugene V. Debs, and Margaret Sanger . . . are its architects as well as Thomas Jefferson and Abraham Lincoln." While not all

American social movements garner popular support or lead to epoch-changing legislation, they each offer their own unique insight into a young democracy's political dialogue.

Each book in Greenhaven's American Social Movements series allows readers to follow the general progression of a particular social movement—examining its historical roots and beginnings in earlier chapters and relatively recent and contemporary information (or even the movement's demise) in later chapters. With the incorporation of both primary and secondary sources, as well as writings by both supporters and critics of the movement, each anthology provides an engaging panoramic view of its subject. Selections include a variety of readings, such as book excerpts, newspaper articles, speeches, manifestos, literary essays, interviews, and personal narratives. The editors of each volume aim to include the voices of movement leaders and participants as well as the opinions of historians, social analysts, and individuals who have been affected by the movement. This comprehensive approach gives students the opportunity to view these movements both as participants have experienced them and as historians and critics have interpreted them.

Every volume in the American Social Movements series includes an introductory essay that presents a broad historical overview of the movement in question. The annotated table of contents and comprehensive index help readers quickly locate material of interest. Each selection is preceded by an introductory paragraph that summarizes the article's content and provides historical context when necessary. Several other research aids are also present, including brief excerpts of supplementary material, a chronology of major events pertaining to the movement, and an accessible bibliography.

The Greenhaven Press American Social Movements series offers readers an informative introduction to some of the most fascinating groups and ideas in American history. The contents of each anthology provide a valuable resource for general readers as well as for enthusiasts of American political science, history, and culture.

INTRODUCTION

In September 1942, scientist Leo Szilard warned, "We cannot have peace in a world in which various sovereign nations have atomic bombs in the possession of their armies and any of these armies could win a war within twenty-four hours after it starts one." Just three years later, on the morning of August 6, 1945, the flash of the first atomic bomb set the course of U.S. nuclear policy.

It would be a whole year before American citizens received firsthand accounts of the effects of the bombing on Japan. John Hershey, then a writer for the *New York Times,* followed six survivors as they made their way throughout that fateful day. Americans read of hellish fires and charred, maimed bodies, yet the majority opinion remained that the use of the atomic bomb was the only way to end the war. A dissenting minority, however, were swayed to channel their outrage into action.

The American antinuclear movement sprang from the actions of concerned scientists like Szilard and pacifist and religious activists who protested the use of the atomic bomb.

AN ATOMIC DISCOVERY

By 1934, the Italian scientist Enrico Fermi had split a uranium atom in two. Four years later, guided by Albert Einstein's formula $E=mc^2$, two exiled German scientists living in Sweden, Lise Meitner and Otto Frisch, achieved atomic fission. On the political front, Adolf Hitler marched his troops into Prague in 1939. It was then that Fermi and Einstein understood the far-reaching consequences of their work: If they did not beat the Nazis to the atomic bomb, the world would suffer. Once they unleashed the bomb, however, how could they ensure that governments would use atomic power only for the benefit of humanity?

Szilard took it upon himself to organize the concerned scientists, many of whom, along with Fermi and Einstein, came to the United States after fleeing the Nazi and fascist regimes. Although the scientific community had always shared research, Szilard persuaded those working on atomic experiments to refrain from publishing their results so that Hitler could not advance his program. In addition, Szilard persuaded Einstein to write President Franklin D. Roosevelt, and on August 2, 1939, Einstein urged FDR to oversee developments in atomic science lest the Nazis achieve a nuclear chain reaction and get to the bomb before the United States. Einstein's urgings led FDR to create the Manhattan Engineering District—the infamous "Manhattan Project"—and set up government-run programs at the Metallurgical Laboratory (Met Lab) at the University of Chicago and in Los Alamos, New Mexico.

In 1941, before Pearl Harbor ushered the United States into World War II, FDR also created an interim advisory committee to brief him on the Manhattan Project. Included on this committee were Vice President Henry A. Wallace, Secretary of War Henry L. Stimson, Army Chief of Staff general George Marshall, and National Academy of Sciences chair Arthur C. Compton. None of the scientists who had voiced their concerns was invited to join the committee. This decision would later be recognized as a symptom of a larger issue: The government was interested in the research but not the opinions of the concerned scientists.

SCIENTISTS LOSE CONTROL OF THEIR CREATION

In May 1945, one month after FDR's death in office, Germany fell and the war in Europe ended. These events excited Szilard and the other scientists over the possibility of ending their development of an atomic bomb and researching instead ways in which nuclear energy could improve the quality of life for all of humanity. The U.S. government, however, disagreed and redoubled efforts to develop an atomic bomb to end the war in the Pacific.

In response, in June 1945, James Franck, Eugene Rabinowitch, Szilard, and several other Met Lab scientists released the "Report of the [Manhattan Project Met Lab] Committee on Political and Social Problems," which attempted to combine their new interests in nuclear energy with the government's desire to bring a swift end to the war in the Pacific. In this report, which came to be called the "Franck Report," the scientists suggested that the bomb be tested on an uninhabited island in the Pacific and not on a populated target because they felt that the demonstration alone would suffice to prompt a Japanese surrender. Then, they continued, the United States could redesign its nuclear program to focus on postwar uses of nuclear energy. The Franck Report was overshadowed, however, by Fermi and J. Robert Oppenheimer, the scientific director of the Los Alamos site, who agreed with FDR's interim committee that only a military demonstration would end the war. Another obstruction—then unknown to the scientists—was that the interim committee had already advised President Harry S. Truman back in May that once they completed the bomb, it must be used on Japan.

On July 16, 1945, the government detonated the first atomic bomb outside of Alamogordo Air Base in New Mexico. According to Fermi, who witnessed the test,

> I had the impression that suddenly the countryside became brighter than in full daylight. I subsequently looked in the direction of the explosion through the dark glass and could see something that looked like a conglomeration of flames that promptly started rising. After a few seconds the rising flames lost their brightness and appeared as a huge pillar of smoke with an expanded head like a gigantic mushroom that rose rapidly beyond the clouds probably to a height of 30,000 feet. After reaching its full height, the smoke stayed stationary for a while before the wind started dissipating it.

The Manhattan Project was on schedule. A time (the beginning of August) and a target were chosen. The interim committee suggested not an uninhabited island, as Szilard and the other concerned scientists had suggested, but a populated city—Hiroshima. The committee also suggested a secondary target—Nagasaki—because it believed that showing that a barrage of such bombs was possible was the only effective means of supporting the first threat.

SOWING THE SEEDS OF DISSENSION

With the Japanese surrender, the U.S. government concluded that the use of the bomb had potentially saved millions of lives, both American and Japanese, and opinion polls showed that most Americans supported this conclusion. However, a small group of dissenters made their voices heard.

Religious pacifists were the first to react. Dorothy Day of the Catholic workers movement denounced the bombings as immoral, and Methodist bishop G. Bromley Oxnam also lamented the indiscriminate obliteration of fellow human beings. They were joined by the Women's International League for Peace and Freedom (WILPF) and the Fellowship of Reconciliation (FOR). Similar reactions on local levels led concerned citizens to mobilize into such grassroots peace organizations as World Peace Research in San Diego, California; the Greater St. Louis Citizens Committee for Nuclear Information; and the St. Louis–based Eves Against Atoms. However, liberal voices were not the only ones raised in protest.

Both Dwight D. Eisenhower, the Allied commander in Europe during World War II, and Douglas MacArthur, the Allied commander in the Pacific, were appalled by the bombing of Japan, as was former president Herbert Hoover. In addition, the *New Yorker,* in an unprecedented response, devoted the entire August 31, 1946, issue to Hershey's account of the effects of the bombing on the city of Hiroshima and its people. The editors' decision was based on their desire for people everywhere to fully realize the implications of the bomb's use. A few did achieve this realization, as shown by letters the editors received. In one letter, a woman bemoans the immorality underlying the actions of America—her homeland—which caused the horrific deaths of civilians, women, and children.

Such antinuclear sentiments were supported on the scientific front by the Atomic Scientists of Chicago, which was formed in 1945 by former Manhattan Project scientists, including Eugene Rabinowitch, who coauthored the Franck Report. By the end of the year, Rabinowitch published the first issue of the *Bulletin of the Atomic Scientists* to raise public awareness of the dangers posed by nuclear weapons and offer better uses for nuclear energy. In 1947, a clock appeared on the *Bulletin's* cover—the infamous "Doomsday Clock"—its hands reading seven minutes to midnight, expressing an apocalyptic fear of what the United States had unleashed on the world.

In 1955, Einstein and noted mathematician and philosopher Bertrand Russell wrote an antinuclear treatise in which they lamented the nondiscriminatory destruction of nuclear war and scientists' lack of understanding the far-reaching effects of even a single explosion. They urged the scientific community to unite and demanded that the United States and Russia enact an immediate nuclear weapons freeze before the fear of not knowing each other's military strength sparked an arms race that led both sides to destruction:

> Although an agreement to renounce nuclear weapons as part of a general reduction of armaments would not afford an ultimate solution, it would serve certain important purposes. First, any agreement between East and West is to the good in so far as it tends to diminish tension. Second, the abolition of thermo-nuclear weapons, if each side believed that the other had carried it out sincerely, would lessen the fear of a sudden attack in the style of Pearl Harbour, which at present keeps both sides in a state of nervous apprehension. We should, therefore, welcome such an agreement though only as a first step.

Einstein died shortly before the treatise's publication, but just two years later, Russell gathered twenty-two scientists from ten countries to convene the first Pugwash Conference on Science and World Affairs to discuss nuclear arms control, a conference that celebrated its fifty-second meeting in August 2002. In these first attempts to influence U.S. nuclear policy, the American antinuclear movement was born.

Yet despite the warnings of the "Russell-Einstein Manifesto," as their antinuclear treatise came to be called, a postwar arms race did develop and became the cornerstone of the Cold War between the United States and Russia. Through the 1950s and 1960s, the tension between these two nations cultivated the public's fear of nuclear war. This, in turn, increased the movement's influence in efforts to freeze nuclear weapons production and parley a freeze into partial disarmament of both U.S. and Russian nuclear arsenals.

NUCLEAR WEAPONS FREEZE AND DISARMAMENT

Although Eisenhower had opposed the atomic bombing of Japan, once he became president, he backed the New Look policy, which held that U.S. nuclear capability was the major Soviet deterrent—psychologically as well as politically. Once the United States and the Soviet Union each had a large enough nuclear arsenal, the policy makers maintained, then a first strike by either side would be highly unlikely. By the beginning of the 1960s, this policy became official military doctrine known as mutual assured destruction (MAD). The fear it created in the American public overpowered any effort by the movement to bring about a nuclear weapons freeze.

In 1952, the United States tested its first hydrogen bomb by detonating it at Enewetak Atoll in the Marshall Islands. Less than a year later, the Russians tested their first nuclear weapon. The arms race was on.

In 1957, Dr. Albert Schweitzer managed to reach several influential public figures with his "Declaration of Conscience" speech, in which he warned of the dangers of nuclear radiation from test detonations. "The end of further experiments with atom bombs," Schweitzer mused, "would be like early sun rays of hope which suffering humanity is longing for." Many of these public figures—writers, editors, and peace activists—put out a call to others willing to confront and attempt to change U.S. nuclear policy. From this beginning rose the

National Committee for a Sane Nuclear Policy (SANE), supported by such luminaries as Schweitzer, Eleanor Roosevelt, Dr. Benjamin Spock, Bertrand Russell, Pablo Casals, and Dr. Martin Luther King Jr.

SANE was a significant voice in the early movement. In 1959, actor Steve Allen hosted the founding meeting of Hollywood SANE, whose high-profile members included Marlon Brando, Henry Fonda, Marilyn Monroe, and Harry Belafonte, and in 1960, a SANE protest rally in New York City's Madison Square Garden attracted twenty thousand people to hear Eleanor Roosevelt, Norman Cousins, Belafonte, and others call for an end to the arms race. Following the Cuban missile crisis in 1962, another SANE rally drew ten thousand supporters, and toward the end of the Vietnam War, SANE organized a protest rally that attracted nearly five hundred thousand people.

Despite the political and military rhetoric of the MAD doctrine, SANE's aggressive advertising to raise public awareness and its backing of political candidates who shared the antinuclear vision contributed to the ratification of the Limited Nuclear Test Ban Treaty in 1963 and the Treaty on the Nonproliferation of Nuclear Weapons in 1968. Such successes paved the way for the Strategic Arms Limitation Talks (SALT) and the Antiballistic Missile (ABM) Treaty of the 1970s, marking the beginning of official consideration of nuclear disarmament. The 1970s, however, also marked the emergence of what the movement perceived as a new threat: nuclear power.

CONFRONTING NUCLEAR POWER

In 1982, Stephen Hilgartner, Richard C. Bell, and Rory O'Connor published a report on the nuclear power industry's "spinning" (that is, making something negative appear positive by manipulating information) in order to sell its power to the public. They dubbed this practice "Nukespeak." For example, they cite numerous instances of the industry's creating favorable impressions in communities near reactors. Before its construction was even completed, Three Mile Island—considered the site of America's worst commercial nuclear accident—had been touted as a "beautifully landscaped" park. Thus, according to the movement, the nuclear power industry brought the promise of nuclear energy to the United States.

On November 13, 1974, Karen Silkwood became the antinuclear movement's first martyr after her car struck a concrete culvert and flipped onto its left side. Had she been forced off the road? This question has prompted numerous investigations since that night that try to discover not only how Silkwood died but also what information she had gathered about her employer, the Kerr-McGee plutonium processing plant in Oklahoma. When she died, Silkwood was on her way to a meeting with her union representative and a *New York Times* journalist to show them her evidence of safety violations that had exposed workers to unacceptable levels of radiation. Although this evidence never surfaced, in 1986, Silkwood's family was finally awarded $1.38 million in punitive damages for Silkwood's own radiation contamination.

TAKING IT TO THE STREETS

In addition to a lack of evidence documenting plant negligence, the movement's political gambles in the nuclear power arena were proving costly and usually unsuccessful (most referenda at the state level did not pass). By contrast, more direct action had stopped the construction of a nuclear power plant in West Germany. Therefore, many grassroots organizations, such as People's Power Project, Society for New Earth, and Mothers for Peace, decided to take their protest to the streets.

In May 1976 at the site of the proposed nuclear power plant in Seabrook, New Hampshire, around two thousand protesters under the lead of the Clamshell Alliance occupied the construction site to focus attention on the planned use of sea water to cool the nuclear reactors. The water, when returned to the ocean, would be hot enough to harm marine life. The protesters, who trained for weeks in nonviolent tactics, carried no weapons and did not fight back when arrested. In fact, they continued their protest even when in custody. They sang, played, and hung their laundry up to dry while the walls of the

New Hampshire national armory bore signs that proclaimed "No Nukes" and "Truth Is Nonviolent."

At the same time, other demonstrations were taking place at construction sites across the country, from San Luis Obispo, California, to Three Mile Island in Pennsylvania. As at Seabrook, protesters at these sites picketed and held teach-ins to raise public awareness about the perils of nuclear power. Construction was often hampered. Then, in 1979, activists' worst fears about nuclear power became reality.

At the Three Mile Island nuclear power plant, about a third of the nuclear fuel melted inside a reactor, and radiation leaked from the power plant into the surrounding areas of central Pennsylvania. Although the report from the President's Commission on the Accident at Three Mile Island made it clear that the "accident was caused by a failure of people, not by malfunctioning equipment," this did little to ease public anxiety, especially the anxiety of the nearly 100 million people who lived within fifty miles of a nuclear power plant.

THE MOVEMENT FINDS STRENGTH IN UNITY

Following the Three Mile Island accident, grassroots groups and larger national organizations began to stage demonstrations together. Groups such as Critical Mass and the New York Public Interest Research Group helped organize a march on Washington to persuade President Jimmy Carter to back down on the U.S. commitment to nuclear power. Dr. Helen Caldicott revived Physicians for Social Responsibility, which later evolved into the International Physicians for the Prevention of Nuclear War (IPPNW), and was awarded the Nobel Peace Prize in 1985 for educating the public about the consequences of nuclear war. And in 1982, 1 million people descended on New York City to protest what they perceived as President Ronald Reagan's pronuclear presidency epitomized by his Strategic Defense Initiative (SDI)—a space-based defense system that would use lasers to shoot down incoming Soviet missiles. SDI never proved feasible, and the media facetiously dubbed it the "Star Wars" project.

The movement's strength was increasing. That same year, Democratic senator Edward M. Kennedy joined with Republican senator Mark O. Hatfield to introduce a resolution that called for a freeze on the testing, production, and further deployment of nuclear warheads, missiles, and other delivery systems within the United States and the Soviet Union. Then, Randall Forsberg, Pam Solo, and Randy Kehler—freeze organization leaders—coordinated with SANE director David Cortright to bring unity to the movement. SANE officially merged with other activist organizations in 1987, undergoing a name change in 1993 to Peace Action.

On June 10, 2001, Project Abolition, a relatively new umbrella organization sponsored by the Fourth Freedom Forum, Peace Action, and IPPNW, among others, held a demonstration in Lafayette Park across from the White House in order to garner support for abolishing the world's nuclear arsenals. According to Project Abolition's mission,

> Through sustained grassroots education and outreach, the project will help to create an informed and active citizen constituency for nuclear weapons abolition. The project will cooperate with all interested individuals and organizations that support the goal of reducing and eliminating nuclear weapons.

The movement's various concerns—nuclear weapons freeze, disarmament, and nuclear power safety—had finally been brought together, a reality echoed in the words of Dr. Caldicott: "As a doctor, as well as a mother and a world citizen, I wish to practice the ultimate form of preventive medicine by ridding the earth of these technologies that propagate disease, suffering, and death."

TODAY'S MOVEMENT

From radiation exposure testing on stillborn fetuses during Project Sunshine in the 1950s, to the high occurrence of various cancers and other genetic damage among those downwind from the Nevada test site during the 1950s and 1960s, to the major nuclear plant "accidents" at Three Mile Island in 1979 and Chernobyl in 1986, to the planned storage of nuclear plant waste in the Yucca Mountains of Nevada in 2005, antinuclear activists wonder, "How many people are expendable?"

There have been several gains, however. Freeze and disarmament measures of previous decades have yielded significant change. The U.S. nuclear arsenal was cut from twenty-three thousand weapons in 1990 to fifteen thousand in 1997. During this same seven-year period, the Russian arsenal was also reduced from thirty-eight thousand weapons to approximately twenty one thousand. In addition, the Union of Concerned Scientists (UCS), which has worked since 1969 to reduce the risks from nuclear power, promote alternatives to nuclear energy, and rid the world of nuclear weapons, has successfully raised public awareness of the Nuclear Regulatory Commission's laxity in enforcing updates and repairs to aging plants, publishing plant-specific risk studies, and improving plant security forces.

Unfortunately, according to David Krieger, founder of the Nuclear Age Peace Foundation, several new issues have developed that demand the movement's immediate attention: keeping nuclear weapons out of the hands of terrorists, achieving elimination of nuclear arsenals as well as nuclear testing for all time, and demonstrating to emerging nuclear powers that a nuclear arsenal is not necessary to national security, that a nuclear weapons–free world is possible. In addition, groups like the UCS are researching renewable energy sources like wind, water, and the sun as alternatives to nuclear power; however, acquiring government support and creating policies at both the state and federal level remain challenges for today's movement.

John A. Simpson, former chairman of the Atomic Scientists of Chicago and another founder of the *Bulletin,* testified in 1945 with other concerned scientists before the U.S. Senate about how nuclear energy under civilian control would benefit humanity. Realizing their moral responsibility as well as their political impotence, these scientists—including Einstein, Szilard, and Rabinowitch—understood that their most significant task would be educating the public and policy makers about the reality of nuclear weapons and nuclear energy. These scientists are aging, however, so Simpson has issued a challenge to the next generation—carry on the fight, a call echoed in the words of warning from David Cortright, former executive director of SANE and current president of the Fourth Freedom Forum: "While the threat of thermonuclear attack on the United States has diminished, the risks of nuclear weapons being used somewhere in the world are probably greater now than at any time in the nuclear age."

To carry on the fight, to meet the new issues of a new millennium, the *Bulletin,* the Nuclear Age Peace Foundation, Project Abolition, Peace Action, Physicians for Social Responsibility, and the UCS have been joined by the Committee on Nuclear Policy, Women's Action for New Directions, and the Coalition to Reduce Nuclear Dangers, currently the largest alliance of international arms control and disarmament groups. Each and every one feels the urgency of the movement's need to confront nuclear weapons and nuclear energy. Following the terrorist attacks on the United States and President George W. Bush's declaration that the ABM Treaty was obsolete, the hands of the *Bulletin of the Atomic Scientists'* Doomsday Clock were moved forward on February 27, 2002, to seven minutes to midnight, the setting at which the clock made its debut. In the words of Jonathan Schell, a leading advocate of nuclear abolition and author of *The Fate of the Earth,* which explores the horrific effects that a nuclear holocaust would have on our planet,

> Absent a coherent global policy that actually does address the new shape of the nuclear predicament, events are likely to be driven in the vicious circle whose operations have already landed us in a world bristling with new nuclear dangers. Continued possession will fuel proliferation; proliferation will fuel hope for missile defense; missile defense

(whether it can work or not) will disrupt arms control; and the disruption of arms control will, completing the circle, fuel proliferation. A second nuclear age has dawned, and it is running out of control.

"How many people are expendable?" This question remains at the heart of the American antinuclear movement.

CHAPTER 1

THE ORIGINS OF THE ANTINUCLEAR MOVEMENT

AMERICAN
SOCIAL
MOVEMENTS

The Pacifist Roots of the Antinuclear Movement

ROBERT D. HOLSWORTH

Robert D. Holsworth traces the roots of antinuclear activism to religious-based pacifism. Pacifists developed the tactics of demonstration and resistance that would later be central to the antinuclear movement at its peak. As the pacifist has a sense of personal responsibility, Holsworth writes, so the activist must as well. This belief was solidified by the Second Vatican Council, which "acknowledged that it was the task of the entire people of God, not just the pope, to contribute to the response which the age demanded." That age—the 1970s—would indeed be a demanding one for the members of the antinuclear movement, but the philosophy of pacifism would show them a way to respond.

Holsworth is the head of the Center for Public Policy at Virginia Commonwealth University, where he also teaches in the political science and public administration department. His areas of expertise include U.S. politics, political theory, and public policy.

C hristian pacifism is one source from which antinuclear political theology draws its ideas. Since the early days of Christianity when many of its converts refused to bear arms for the Roman Empire, pacifism has periodically surfaced as a response to the war-making tendencies of political entities. In modern America, pacifism has been associated most frequently with the so-called historic peace churches—the Quakers, the Mennonites, and the Church of the Brethren—and with the Jehovah's Witnesses. On many occasions, pacifists have not posed a direct challenge to the state insofar as they concentrated primarily on obtaining recognition for their beliefs and eschewed working to change the political order. At times, however, pacifism has become a dissident ideology as its supporters have sought to imbue the political world with its principles. Pacifists have thus been active in numerous antiwar movements and have also seen fit to apply their ideas about human rights and the dignity of all people to related causes. In American society, pacifists were prominent in the abolitionist crusade, in the early days of the civil rights movement, in prison reform, and in agitation against capital punishment.

Religious pacifists have always been part of the antinuclear weapons movement in the United States. During World War II, pacifists who had accepted the option of alternative service were placed in Civilian Public Service (CPS) camps. Many of those who declined spent the war years in prison. At this time, the magazine *Fellowship* was one of the principal organs of pacifist communication. Edited by A.J. Muste for the Fellowship of Reconciliation, its twin foci during the war were conditions in the CPS camps and the prisons and the imperative of bringing the fighting to a negotiated conclusion. *Fellowship* had opposed the war on the classical pacifist ground that it was immoral to kill other human beings, but it had also maintained that technological advances made it increasingly difficult to legitimate war according to traditional just-war theory. Muste furnished a running commentary on the totalistic and nondiscriminatory nature of modern warfare. He felt that the obliteration bombing conducted by the Allies was a perfect example of how the "just participant" was compelled to match, if not outdo, the evil of the original aggressor. When the fighting was terminated with the bombings of Hiroshima and Nagasaki, *Fellowship* viewed it as devastating proof of its assertions, a cosmic disturbance calling for universal repentance.

In the years immediately following the war, religious pacifists became active in the initial movement to control atomic weaponry, a crusade whose most celebrated participants were the atomic scientists themselves. Arguing against [American clergyman and theologian] Reinhold Niebuhr's contention that political behavior could not be patterned on the model of individual morality, Muste contended that Christians were called to give witness to their belief in ways that could help to establish the Kingdom of God on earth. He believed that atomic weapons were the culmination of a trend in modern technological societies which had rendered human life increasingly meaningless. Prefiguring some of the arguments that were to be central to the work of social critics such as Jacques Ellul and Herbert Marcuse, Muste wrote that "we live in an age where the individual is in danger of becoming a cipher. He is overwhelmed by the vast and intricate technological machinery around which he is increasingly dependent and by which he is increasingly regimented in peace and war." In the face of this centralized, technological juggernaut, Muste implored individuals to take responsibility for the fate of the world, to reassert the claims of conscience against those who would find such statements naive and idealistic. The assumption of personal responsibility was, for Muste, a paradigmatic act that symbolized the character transformation and moral courage required for genuine disarmament. "It is the individual conscience against the atomic bomb which constitutes our sole safeguard."

Dorothy Day and others in the Catholic Worker movement concurred with the personalist orientation of Muste's pacifism. She felt that it was critical for individuals to learn how to "say no" to the powerful when their dictates violated individual conscience and the message of the gospel. Day insisted that this no-saying be connected to personal humility and a serving demeanor. People in the Catholic Worker movement rejected forms of radicalism in which commitment to structural change was not complemented and tempered by merciful activities. They believed that work on behalf of peace and social justice ought to be rooted in the personal lives of activists who followed the plain but demanding gospel commands not to kill, but to feed the hungry, clothe the naked, and shelter the homeless. The distinctive contribution of Day and the

Catholic Worker activists was their attribution of importance to community, underscoring the notion that social change was best undertaken by people who were part of communities of resistance and reconstruction—witnessing to injustice, ministering to the disadvantaged, and embodying a living alternative to mainstream America.

PERSONAL AND COMMUNAL RESISTANCE

The political implications of the pacifist stance were not always precisely enunciated. In their heart of hearts, pacifists hoped that the United States might see fit [following World War II] to send a letter to the Soviet Union noting that "we are through with war and preparation for war. We hope you are too and that we may have universal disarmament. But whether you join us or not, we are through. War simply does not make sense any more. . . . We shall do the best we can to secure ourselves against attack. Knowing how desperately poor the rest of the world is, we shall be prepared to share with others a good deal of the resources God has given us. . . . Anyway we prefer giving it away to spending it on atom bombs and death rays. What is left for ourselves we shall enjoy in peace and quietness during the few years that remain to us and our children." Barring the realization of this dream, pacifists became involved in the forties and fifties in a number of campaigns against nuclear weapons. They called for international control of atomic energy and were active in pursuing a test ban. They advocated personal and communal resistance to the nuclear arms race. They engaged in tax resistance; they participated in sit-ins during public evacuations; and they entered testing areas to dramatize their opposition to the further refinement of nuclear weaponry. Far outside the political mainstream in the forties and early fifties, their direct influence was slight. But they were to become key participants in the civil rights struggles of the fifties and they had developed tactics of resistance that were to be central elements of the antiwar protests and the antinuclear agitation of later years.

A second source of antinuclear political theology has been

evangelical reformism and radicalism. This statement may appear curious because evangelism is today principally associated with personal religion and political conservatism. Historically, however, this has not always been the case, as the quest for personal holiness and the desire to lead a sanctified life were not divorced from an active engagement with the world. Inspired by a burning earnestness, numerous nineteenth-century reformers combined their quest for salvation with campaigns to eliminate evil in the wider society. In the antislavery, labor reform, and temperance campaigns, they often set their hopes quite high, calling for changes more far-reaching than those endorsed by the typical reformer of the twentieth century. While entreating the individual sinner to repent, they also desired to usher in the millennium. As [academic] Timothy Smith has pointed out, "The evangelist played a key role in the widespread attack upon slavery, poverty and greed. They thus helped prepare the way in both theory and practice for what later became known as the social gospel."...

CHALLENGING TRADITION

The United States Catholic Church's gradual working out of the implications of the Second Vatican Council has been a third source of antinuclear political theology. In the early sixties, Vatican II contributed to a reorientation of the Church's teachings on social issues, a body of thought known since [Pope] Leo XIII's *Rerum Novarum* [Concerning Revolutionary Change] encyclical of 1891 as Catholic Social Doctrine. Until the Second Vatican Council, Catholic Social Doctrine was in large measure characterized by its hierarchical formation, abstract tone, and lack of direct challenge to the policies of Western capitalist democracies. It was defined almost exclusively by the pope's pronouncements on social and political issues, rather than by the outcome of a process of discussion and debate among the members of the Church community. Moreover, while the popes did side with the laboring masses and the poor in opposition to the most heartless capitalist practices, their statements were as often intended to combat the appeal of socialism as they were to criticize the inequities of capitalism. In the United States, the modest critical thrust of Catholic Social Doctrine was further blunted by the hierarchy's interest in assimilating the Church into the culture as a way of avoiding nativist attacks on its alien nature.

Vatican II supplied a way of looking at the world that altered the traditional emphases. John XXIII had spoken of the need for the Church to discern what he called the spirit of the times, a spirit he observed in the demands for freedom and dignity being raised by the poor, by women, and by the colonized peoples of the globe. As [researcher] Peter Hebblethwaite has written, "No longer does Catholic Social Doctrine simply parachute principles down from great height. Instead, it takes the hopes and aspirations that people really have and reads in them a message from the Holy Spirit." Furthermore, while the Second Vatican Council reserved a special place for pastors and theologians in the interpretation of these signs, it acknowledged that it was the task of the entire people of God, not just the pope, to contribute to the response which the age demanded.

THE ENDURANCE OF MORAL ACTIVISM

With respect to issues of war and peace, the Second Vatican Council reiterated the condemnations of total war which had been issued by recent popes. The council noted first that "any act of war aimed indiscriminately at the destruction of entire cities or of extensive areas along with their population is a crime against God and man himself. It merits unequivocal and unhesitating condemnation." The council then proceeded to criticize the arms race as a deceitful method for keeping the peace which, in the short term, robbed the poor and, in the long run, undermined the possibility of genuine peace. "The arms race is a treacherous trap for humanity, and one which injures the poor to an intolerable degree. It is much to be feared that if this race persists, it will eventually spawn all the lethal ruin whose path it is now making ready." Finally, it urged both nations and individual Christians to "strain every muscle" to prevent nuclear war and to bring a new cooperativeness and civility to international politics.

In this country, Vatican II ushered in a period of experimentation, examination, and controversy. For many Catholics, its initial effects were experienced in liturgical changes and the abandonment of certain traditional regulations. People debated whether it was better to hear the Mass in English, whether it was preferable to have the priest face the congregation, and whether it was good that Catholics could now eat meat on Friday. But as time passed, the council's broader implications became apparent. The American bishops agonized over their stance toward the U.S. involvement in Vietnam, moving as a body from qualified approval in 1966 to an oppositional posture by the early seventies. During the seventies, the turmoil in Latin America and the controversies in which the Church was embroiled there led numerous American Catholics to become more interested in international affairs at precisely the moment when many cultural observers were lamenting the inward, narcissistic turn of the American population.

Voices of Dissent: Manhattan Project Scientists Address Arms Control and Scientific Responsibility

JAMES FRANCK ET AL.

The war in Europe ended in May 1945; however, the war in the Pacific continued with no end in sight, which gave the American government new motivation to develop the atomic bomb. In June 1945 several scientists working at the Manhattan Project's Metallurgical Laboratory (Met Lab) at the University of Chicago were appointed by the Met Lab director to form the Committee on Social and Political Implications of Atomic Energy. On June 11, barely two months before America bombed Hiroshima, these scientists—James Franck, Donald J. Hughes, J.J. Nickson, Eugene Rabinowitch, Glenn T. Seaborg, J.C. Stearns, and Leo Szilard—produced a report in which they argued against a military demonstration of the atomic bomb. They instead urged the American government to detonate the bomb in the desert or on a barren island, which they believed would be an adequate warning to the Japanese, and they stressed the need for an international agreement to regulate the use of atomic energy to prevent a postwar arms race.

The report went unheeded by both fellow scientists and the American government. In an effort to address these implications, the War Department created the Interim Committee in May 1945,

Excerpted from "Report of the Committee on Political and Social Problems, Manhattan Project 'Metallurgical Laboratory,'" by J. Franck et al. (Washington, DC: U.S. National Archives, 1945).

which included the secretary of war, Henry L. Stimson, as well as several top military leaders and scientists. On May 31, weeks before the Franck Report was published, the committee had already decided to drop the atomic bomb on Hiroshima.

These concerned scientists came to the realization that if they could not sway colleagues or their own government, then they would have to take their message to the people. Eugene Rabinowitch cofounded the *Bulletin of the Atomic Scientists*, a journal dedicated to educating citizens about the continuing dangers of nuclear weapons. This journal initially was the only forum in which these scientists could voice their objections to the emerging U.S. nuclear policy. In addition, Leo Szilard inspired the creation of the Council for a Livable World, an arms control and disarmament group, and many of these scientists participated in the first meetings of the Pugwash Conference, an annual gathering of scientists from the international community that addresses arms control and disarmament as well as scientific responsibility.

I t could be suggested that the danger of destruction by nuclear weapons can be prevented—at least as far as this country is concerned—by keeping our discoveries secret for an indefinite time, or by developing our nucleonic armaments at such a pace that no other nations would think of attacking us from fear of overwhelming retaliation.

The answer to the first suggestion is that although we undoubtedly are at present ahead of the rest of the world in this field, the fundamental facts of nuclear power are a subject of common knowledge. British scientists know as much as we do about the basic war time progress of nucleonics—with the exception of specific processes used in our engineering developments—and the background of French nuclear physicists plus their occasional contact with our Projects, will enable them to catch up rapidly, at least as far as basic scientific facts are concerned. German scientists, in whose discoveries the whole development of this field has originated, apparently did not develop it during the war to the same extent to which this has been done in America; but to the last day of the European war, we have been living in constant apprehension as to their possible achievements. The knowledge that German scientists were working on this weapon and that their government certainly had no scruples against using it when available, was the main motivation of the initiative which American scientists have taken in developing nuclear power on such a large scale for military use in this country. In Russia, too, the basic facts and implications of nuclear power were well understood in 1940, and the experiences of Russian scientists in nuclear research is entirely sufficient to enable them to retrace our steps within a few years, even if we would make all attempts to conceal them. Furthermore, we should not expect too much success from attempts to keep basic information secret in peace time, when scientists acquainted with the work on this and associated Projects will be scattered to many colleges and research institutions and many of them will continue to work on problems closely related to those on which our developments are based. In other words, even if we can retain our leadership in basic knowledge of nucleonics for a certain time by maintaining the secrecy of all results achieved on this and associated Projects, it would be foolish to hope that this can protect us for more than a few years. . . .

One could further ask whether we cannot feel ourselves safe in a race of nuclear armaments by virtue of our greater industrial potential, including greater diffusion of scientific and technical knowledge, greater volume and efficiency of our skilled labor corps, and greater experience of our management—all the factors whose importance has been so strikingly demonstrated in the conversion of this country into an arsenal of the Allied Nations in the present war. The answer is that all that these advantages can give us, is the accumulation of a larger number of bigger and better atomic bombs—and this only if we produce those bombs at the maximum of our capacity in peace time, and do not rely on conversion of a peace time nucleonics industry to military production after the beginning of hostilities.

However, such a quantitative advantage in reserves of bottled destructive power will not make us safe from sudden attack. Just because a potential enemy will be afraid of being "outnumbered and outgunned," the temptation for him may be overwhelming to attempt a sudden unprovoked blow—particularly if he would suspect us of harboring aggressive intentions against his security or "sphere of influence." In no other type of warfare does the advantage lie so heavily with the aggressor. He can place his "infernal machines" in advance in all our major cities and explode them simultaneously, thus destroying a major part of our industry and killing a large proportion of our population, aggregated in densely populated metropolitan districts. Our possibilities of retaliation—even if retaliation would be considered compensation for the loss of tens of millions of lives and destruction of our largest cities—will be greatly handicapped because we must rely on aerial transportation of the bombs, particularly if we would have to deal with an enemy whose industry and population are dispersed over a large territory.

In fact, if the race of nuclear armaments is allowed to develop, the only apparent way in which our country could be protected from the paralyzing effects of a sudden attack is by dispersal of industries which are essential for our war effort and dispersal of the population of our major metropolitan cities. As long as nuclear bombs remain scarce (this will be the case until uranium and thorium cease to be the only basic materials for their fabrication) efficient dispersal of our industry and the scattering of our metropolitan population will considerably decrease the temptation of attacking us by nuclear weapons. . . .

UNVEILING THE BOMB

The prospect of nuclear warfare and the type of measures which have to be taken to protect a country from total destruction by nuclear bombing, must be as abhorrent to other nations as to the United States. England, France, and the smaller nations of the European continent, with their congeries of people and industries, are in an entirely hopeless situation in the face of such a threat. Russia and China are the only great nations which could survive a nuclear attack. However, even though these countries value human life less than the peoples of Western Europe and America, and even though Russia, in particular, has an immense space over which its vital industries could be dispersed and a government which can order this dispersion, the day it is convinced that such a measure is necessary—there is no doubt that Russia, too, will shudder at the possibility of a sudden disintegration of Moscow and Leningrad, almost miraculously preserved in the present war, and of its new industrial sites in the Urals and Siberia. Therefore, only lack of mutual *trust,* and not lack of *desire* for agreement, can stand in the path of an efficient agreement for the prevention of nuclear warfare.

From this point of view, the way in which nuclear weapons, now secretly developed in this country, will first be revealed to the world appears of great, perhaps fateful importance.

One possible way—which may particularly appeal to those who consider the nuclear bombs primarily as a secret weapon developed to help win the present war—is to use it without warning on an appropriately selected object in Japan. It is doubtful whether the first available bombs, of comparatively low efficiency and small size, will be sufficient to break the will or ability of Japan to resist, especially given the fact that the major cities like Tokyo, Nagoya, Osaka, and Kobe already will largely be reduced to ashes by the slower process of ordinary aerial bombing. . . . It will be very difficult to persuade the world that a nation which was capable of secretly preparing and suddenly releasing a weapon, as indiscriminate as the rocket bomb and a thousand times more destructive, is to be trusted in its proclaimed desire of having such weapons abolished by international agreement. We have large accumulations of poison gas, but do not use them, and recent polls have shown that public opinion in this country would disapprove of such a use even if it would accelerate the winning of the Far Eastern war. It is true, that some irrational element in mass psychology makes gas poisoning more revolting than blasting by explosive, even though gas warfare is in no way more "inhuman" than the war of bombs and bullets. Nevertheless, it is not at all certain that the American public opinion, if it could be enlightened as to the effect of atomic explosives, would support the first introduction by our own country of such an indiscriminate method of wholesale destruction of civilian life.

AN APPEAL TO REASON

Thus, from the "optimistic" point of view—looking forward to an international agreement on prevention of nuclear warfare—the military advantages and the saving of American lives, achieved by the sudden use of atomic bombs against Japan, may be outweighed by the ensuing loss of confidence and wave of horror and repulsion, sweeping over the rest of the world, and perhaps dividing even the public opinion at home.

From this point of view a demonstration of the new weapon may best be made before the eyes of representatives of all United Nations, on the desert or a barren island. The best possible atmosphere for the achievement of an international agreement could be achieved if America would be able to say to the world, "You see what weapon we had but did not use. We are ready to renounce its use in the future and to join other nations in working out adequate supervision of the use of this nuclear weapon."...

After such a demonstration the weapon could be used against Japan if a sanction of the United Nations (and of the public opinion at home) could be obtained, perhaps after a preliminary ultimatum to Japan to surrender or at least to evacuate a certain region as an alternative to the total destruction of this target. . . .

The benefit to the nation, and the saving of American lives in the future, achieved by renouncing an early demonstration of nuclear bombs and letting the other nations come into the race only reluctantly, on the basis of guesswork and without definite knowledge that the "thing does work," may far outweigh the advantages to be gained by the immediate use of the first and comparatively inefficient bombs in the war against Japan. At the least, pros and cons of this use must be carefully weighed by the supreme political and military leadership of the country, and the decision should not be left to considerations, merely, of military tactics.

One may point out that the scientists themselves have initiated the development of this "secret weapon" and it is therefore strange that they should be reluctant to try it out on the enemy as soon as it is available. The answer to this question was given above—the compelling reason for creating this weapon with such speed was our fear that Germany had the technical skill necessary to develop such a weapon without any moral constraints regarding its use.

Another argument which could be quoted in favor of using atomic bombs as soon as they are available is that so much taxpayers' money has been invested in these Projects that the Congress and the American public will require a return for their money. The above-mentioned attitude of the American public opinion in the question of the use of poison gas against Japan shows that one can expect it to understand that a weapon can sometimes be made ready only for use in extreme emergency; and as soon as the potentialities of nuclear weapons will be revealed to the American people, one can be certain that it will support all attempts to make the use of such weapons impossible.

Once this is achieved, the large installations and the accumulation of explosive materials at present earmarked for potential military use, will become available for important peace time developments, including power production, large engineering undertakings, and mass production of radioactive materials. In this way, the money spent on war time development of nucleonics may become a boon for the peace time development of national economy. . . .

Given mutual trust and willingness on all sides to give up a certain part of their sovereign rights, by admitting international control of certain phases of national economy, the control could be exercised (alternatively or simultaneously) on two different levels.

The first and perhaps simplest way is to ration the raw materials—primarily, the uranium ores. Production of nuclear explosives begins with processing of large quantities of uranium in large isotope separation plants or huge production piles. The amounts of ore taken out of the ground at different locations could be controlled by resident agents of the international Control Board, and each nation could be allotted only an amount which would make large scale separation of fissionable isotopes impossible. . . .

An agreement on a higher level, involving more mutual trust and understanding, would be to allow unlimited production, but keep exact bookkeeping on the fate of each pound of uranium mined. Certain difficulty with this method of control will arise in the second stage of production, when one pound of pure fissionable isotope will be used again and again to produce additional fissionable material from thorium. These could perhaps be overcome by extending control to the mining and use of thorium, even though the commercial use of this metal may cause complications.

If check is kept on the conversion of uranium and thorium ore into pure fissionable materials, the question arises how to prevent accumulation of large quantities of such material in the hands of one or several nations. Accumulations of this kind could be rapidly converted into atomic bombs if a nation would break away from international control. It has been suggested that a compulsory denaturation of pure fissionable isotopes may be agreed upon—they should be diluted after production by suitable isotopes to make them useless for military purposes (except if purified by a process whose development must take two or three years), while retaining their usefulness for power engines.

One thing is clear: any international agreement on prevention of nuclear armaments must be backed by actual and efficient controls. No paper agreement can be sufficient since neither this or any other nation can stake its whole existence on trust into other nations' signatures. Every attempt to impede the international control agencies must be considered equivalent to denunciation of the agreement.

It hardly needs stressing that we as scientists believe that any systems of controls envisaged should leave as much freedom for the peace development of nucleonics as is consistent with the safety of the world.

An Antinuclear, Antiwar Manifesto

ALBERT EINSTEIN AND BERTRAND RUSSELL

Albert Einstein and Bertrand Russell—both scientists and outspoken critics of the first U.S. nuclear agenda—moved generations of Americans to join the antinuclear movement. From the beginning of the nuclear age, these men strove to sway political policy and public opinion as to the threat nuclear weapons posed to humanity.

In 1931 Einstein urged scientists not to work on military assignments, and when the Manhattan Project was created, he took no part in it. Not once but twice he tried to warn President Franklin D. Roosevelt about unleashing the horror of nuclear war on the world and about the need for international cooperation to avoid a postwar arms race. After World War II Russell organized the first Pugwash Conference—an international symposium on nuclear disarmament and scientific responsibility—and founded the Campaign for Nuclear Disarmament. In 1961 he was imprisoned for his involvement with antinuclear protests.

Ten years after the U.S. atomic bombing of Japan, Einstein and Russell cowrote the following antinuclear treatise that has become the cornerstone of the antinuclear movement. In it, they lament the nondiscriminatory destruction of nuclear war as foreshadowed by Hiroshima and Nagasaki, and they contend that hydrogen bomb tests reveal that scientists do not understand the far-reaching effects of even a single explosion. Therefore, Einstein and Russell urge the scientific community to unite—which happens two years later at the first Pugwash Conference—and to demand that the president enact an immediate nuclear weapons freeze, leading eventually to the disarmament of world arsenals and to an abolition of war itself—the only solution they can imagine to avoid humanity's extinction.

I n the tragic situation which confronts humanity, we feel that scientists should assemble in conference to appraise the perils that have arisen as a result of the development of weapons of mass destruction, and to discuss a resolution in the spirit of the appended draft.

We are speaking on this occasion [at a press conference on July 9, 1955], not as members of this or that nation, continent, or creed, but as human beings, members of the species Man, whose continued existence is in doubt. The world is full of conflicts; and, overshadowing all minor conflicts, the titanic struggle between Communism and anti-Communism.

Almost everybody who is politically conscious has strong feelings about one or more of these issues; but we want you, if you can, to set aside such feelings and consider yourselves only as members of a biological species which has had a remarkable history, and whose disappearance none of us can desire.

We shall try to say no single word which should appeal to one group rather than to another. All, equally, are in peril, and, if the peril is understood, there is hope that they may collectively avert it.

THE FAR-REACHING DESTRUCTION OF NUCLEAR WAR

We have to learn to think in a new way. We have to learn to ask ourselves, not what steps can be taken to give military victory to whatever group we prefer, for there no longer are such steps; the question we have to ask ourselves is: what steps can be taken to prevent a military contest of which the issue must be disastrous to all parties?

The general public, and even many men in positions of authority, have not realized what would be involved in a war with nuclear bombs. The general public still thinks in terms of the obliteration of cities. It is understood that the new bombs are more powerful than the old, and that, while one A-bomb [atomic bomb] could obliterate Hiroshima, one H-bomb [hydrogen bomb] could obliterate the largest cities, such as London, New York, and Moscow.

Scientists Unite to Avoid a Nuclear Holocaust

We invite this Congress, and through it the scientists of the world and the general public, to subscribe to the following resolution:

"In view of the fact that in any future world war nuclear weapons will certainly be employed, and that such weapons threaten the continued existence of mankind, we urge the Governments of the world to realize, and to acknowledge publicly, that their purpose cannot be furthered by a world war, and we urge them, consequently, to find peaceful means for the settlement of all matters of dispute between them."

Max Born et al. Press release July 9, 1955.

No doubt in an H-bomb war great cities would be obliterated. But this is one of the minor disasters that would have to be faced. If everybody in London, New York, and Moscow were exterminated, the world might, in the course of a few centuries, recover from the blow. But we now know, especially since the Bikini [Atoll] test, that nuclear bombs can gradually spread destruction over a very much wider area than had been supposed.

It is stated on very good authority that a bomb can now be manufactured which will be 2,500 times as powerful as that which destroyed Hiroshima. Such a bomb, if exploded near the ground or under water, sends radio-active particles into the upper air. They sink gradually and reach the surface of the earth in the form of a deadly dust or rain. It was this dust which infected the Japanese fishermen and their catch of fish.

SHALL WE ABOLISH WAR—OR HUMANITY?

No one knows how widely such lethal radio-active particles might be diffused, but the best authorities are unanimous in saying that a war with H-bombs might possibly put an end to the human race. It is feared that if many H-bombs are used there will be universal death, sudden only for a minority, but for the majority a slow torture of disease and disintegration.

Many warnings have been uttered by eminent men of science and by authorities in military strategy. None of them will say that the worst results are certain. What they do say is that these results are possible, and no one can be sure that they will not be realized. We have not yet found that the views of experts on this question depend in any degree upon their politics or prejudices. They depend only, so far as our researches have revealed, upon the extent of the particular expert's knowledge. We have found that the men who know most are the most gloomy.

Here, then, is the problem which we present to you, stark and dreadful and inescapable: Shall we put an end to the human race; or shall mankind renounce war? People will not face this alternative because it is so difficult to abolish war.

THE FIRST STEP: A NUCLEAR WEAPONS FREEZE

The abolition of war will demand distasteful limitations of national sovereignty. But what perhaps impedes understanding of the situation more than anything else is that the term "mankind" feels vague and abstract. People scarcely realize in imagination that the danger is to themselves and their children and their grandchildren, and not only to a dimly apprehended humanity. They can scarcely bring themselves to grasp that they, individually, and those whom they love are in imminent danger of perishing agonizingly. And so they hope that perhaps war may be allowed to continue provided modern weapons are prohibited.

This hope is illusory. Whatever agreements not to use H-bombs had been reached in time of peace, they would no longer be considered binding in time of war, and both sides would set to work to manufacture H-bombs as soon as war broke out, for, if one side manufactured the bombs and the other did not, the side that manufactured them would inevitably be victorious.

Although an agreement to renounce nuclear weapons as part of a general reduction of armaments would not afford an ultimate solution, it would serve certain important purposes. First: any agreement between East and West is to the good in so far as it tends to diminish tension. Second: the abolition of thermo-nuclear weapons, if each side believed that the other had carried it out sincerely, would lessen the fear of a sudden attack in the style of Pearl Harbour, which at present keeps both sides in a state of nervous apprehension. We should, therefore, welcome such an agreement though only as a first step.

REMEMBER HUMANITY AND FORGET THE REST

Most of us are not neutral in feeling, but, as human beings, we have to remember that, if the issues between East and West are to be decided in any manner that can give any possible satisfaction to anybody, whether Communist or anti-Communist, whether Asian or European or American, whether White or Black, then these issues must not be decided by war. We should wish this to be understood, both in the East and in the West.

There lies before us, if we choose, continual progress in happiness, knowledge, and wisdom. Shall we, instead, choose death, because we cannot forget our quarrels? We appeal, as human beings, to human beings: Remember your humanity, and forget the rest. If you can do so, the way lies open to a new Paradise; if you cannot, there lies before you the risk of universal death.

Inspiring a
Movement: *Hiroshima*

JOHN HERSHEY

John Hershey approved of the atomic bombing of Japan. Then he traveled to Hiroshima and recorded the effects of the bombing by reenacting the event through the eyes of six survivors. His approval turned to horror, and Hershey in turn relayed his feelings to the American people through the publication of his thirty thousand–word account, *Hiroshima*, on CBS radio, in national newspapers, and in the entire August 31, 1946, issue of the *New Yorker*. The impact was immediate.

A letter to the editor of the *New Yorker* deftly represented the minority opinion of moral outrage: "As I read I had to constantly remind myself that we perpetrated this monstrous tragedy. We Americans." Unfortunately, most Americans at the time supported the bombing, and for them *Hiroshima* only reinforced the sociopolitical power behind the bomb. Once the antinuclear movement began to take shape, however, this narrative of destruction, this proof of the bomb's horrific potential, inspired the creation of countless activists and organizations dedicated to nuclear disarmament and the preservation of the human race.

The following excerpt begins directly after the bomb has dropped and before anyone on the ground knew exactly what had befallen them.

All day, people poured into Asano Park. This private estate was far enough away from the explosion so that its bamboos, pines, laurel, and maples were still alive, and the green place invited refugees—partly because they believed that if the Americans came back, they would bomb only buildings; partly because the foliage seemed a center of coolness and life, and the estate's exquisitely precise rock gardens, with their quiet pools and arching bridges, were very Japanese, normal, secure; and also partly (according to some who were there) because of an irresistible, atavistic urge to hide under leaves. Mrs. Nakamura and her children were among the first to arrive, and they settled in the bamboo grove near the river. They all felt terribly thirsty, and they drank from the river. At once they were nauseated and began vomiting, and they retched the whole day. Others were also nauseated; they all thought (probably because of the strong odor of ionization, an "electric smell" given off by the bomb's fission) that they were sick from a gas the Americans had dropped. When Father Kleinsorge and the other priests came into the park, nodding to their friends as they passed, the Nakamuras were all sick and prostrate. A woman named Iwasaki, who lived in the neighborhood of the mission and who was sitting near the Nakamuras, got up and asked the priests if she should stay where she was or go with them. Father Kleinsorge said, "I hardly know where the safest place is." She stayed there, and later in the day, though she had no visible wounds or burns, she died. The priests went farther along the river and settled down in some underbrush. Father LaSalle lay down and went right to sleep. The theological student, who was wearing slippers, had carried with him a bundle of clothes, in which he had packed two pairs of leather shoes. When he sat down with the others, he found that the bundle had broken open and a couple of shoes had fallen out and now he had only two lefts. He retraced his steps and found one right. When he rejoined the priests, he said, "It's funny, but things don't matter any more. Yesterday, my shoes were my most important possessions. Today, I don't care. One pair is enough."

Father Cieslik said, "I know. I started to bring my books along, and then I thought, 'This is no time for books.'"

When Mr. Tanimoto, with his basin still in his hand, reached the park, it was very crowded, and to distinguish the living from the dead was not easy, for most of the people lay still, with their eyes open. To Father Kleinsorge, an Occidental, the silence in the grove by the river, where hundreds of gruesomely wounded suffered together, was one of the most dreadful and awesome phenomena of his whole experience. The hurt ones were quiet; no one wept, much less screamed in pain; no one complained; none of the many who died did so noisily; not even the children cried; very few people even spoke. And when Father Kleinsorge gave water to some whose faces had been almost blotted out by flash burns, they took their share and then raised themselves a little and bowed to him, in thanks.

DISTURBING THE DEAD TO SAVE THE LIVING

Mr. Tanimoto greeted the priests and then looked around for other friends. He saw Mrs. Matsumoto, wife of the director of the Methodist School, and asked her if she was thirsty. She was, so he went to one of the pools in the Asanos' rock gardens and got water for her in his basin. Then he decided to try to get back to his church. He went into Nobori-cho by the way the priests had taken as they escaped, but he did not get far; the fire along the streets was so fierce that he had to turn back. He walked to the riverbank and began to look for a boat in which he might carry some of the most severely injured across the river from Asano Park and away from the spreading fire. Soon he found a good-sized pleasure punt drawn up on the bank, but in and around it was an awful tableau—five dead men, nearly naked, badly burned, who must have expired more or less all at once, for they were in attitudes which suggested that they had been working together to push the boat down into the river. Mr. Tanimoto lifted them away from the boat, and as he did so, he experienced such horror at disturbing the dead—preventing them, he momentarily felt, from launching their craft and going on their ghostly way—that he said out loud, "Please forgive me for taking this boat. I must use it for others, who are alive." The punt was heavy, but he managed to slide it into the water. There were no oars, and all he could find for propulsion was a thick bamboo pole. He worked the boat upstream to the most crowded part of the park and began to ferry the wounded. He could pack ten or twelve into the boat for each crossing, but as the river was too deep in the center to pole his way across, he had to paddle with the bamboo, and consequently each trip took a very long time. He worked several hours that way.

Early in the afternoon, the fire swept into the woods of Asano Park. The first Mr. Tanimoto knew of it was when, returning in his boat, he saw that a great number of people had moved toward the riverside. On touching the bank, he went up to investigate, and when he saw the fire, he shouted, "All the young men who are not badly hurt come with me!" Father Kleinsorge moved Father Schiffer and Father LaSalle close to the edge of the river and asked people there to get them across if the fire came too near, and then joined Tanimoto's volunteers. Mr. Tanimoto sent some to look for buckets and basins and told others to beat the burning underbrush with their clothes; when utensils were at hand, he formed a bucket chain from one of the pools in the rock gardens. The team fought the fire for more than two hours, and gradually defeated the flames. As Mr. Tanimoto's men worked, the frightened people in the park pressed closer and closer to the river, and finally the mob began to force some of the unfortunates who were on the very bank into the water. Among those driven into the river and drowned were Mrs. Matsumoto, of the Methodist School, and her daughter.

FEAR AND CONFUSION

When Father Kleinsorge got back after fighting the fire, he found Father Schiffer still bleeding and terribly pale. Some Japanese stood around and stared at him, and Father Schiffer whispered, with a weak smile, "It is as if I were already dead." "Not yet," Father Kleinsorge said. He had brought Dr. Fujii's first-aid kit with him, and he had noticed Dr. Kanda in the crowd, so he sought him out and asked him if he would dress Father Schiffer's bad cuts. Dr. Kanda had seen his wife and daughter dead in the ruins of his hospital; he sat now with his head in his hands. "I can't do anything," he said. Father Kleinsorge bound more bandage around Father Schiffer's head, moved him to a steep place, and settled him so that his head was high, and soon the bleeding diminished.

The roar of approaching planes was heard about this time. Someone in the crowd near the Nakamura family shouted, "It's some Grummans coming to strafe us!" A baker named Nakashima stood up and commanded, "Everyone who is wearing anything white, take it off." Mrs. Nakamura took the blouses off her children, and opened her umbrella and made them get under it. A great number of people, even badly burned ones, crawled into bushes and stayed there until the hum, evidently of a reconnaissance or weather run, died away.

It began to rain. Mrs. Nakamura kept her children under the umbrella. The drops grew abnormally large, and someone shouted, "The Americans are dropping gasoline. They're going to set fire to us!" (This alarm stemmed from one of the theories being passed through the park as to why so much of Hiroshima had burned: it was that a single plane had sprayed gasoline on the city and then somehow set fire to it in one flashing moment.) But the drops were palpably water, and as they fell, the wind grew stronger and stronger, and suddenly—probably because of the tremendous convection set up by the blazing city—a whirlwind ripped through the park. Huge trees crashed down; small ones were uprooted and flew into the air. Higher, a wild array of flat things revolved in the twisting funnel—pieces of iron roofing, papers, doors, strips of matting. Father Kleinsorge put a piece of cloth over Father Schiffer's eyes, so that the feeble man would not think he was going crazy. The gale blew Mrs. Murata, the mission housekeeper, who was sitting close by the river, down the embankment at a shallow, rocky place, and she came out with her bare feet bloody. The vortex moved out onto the river, where it sucked up a waterspout and eventually spent itself.

VENTURING INTO GROUND ZERO

After the storm, Mr. Tanimoto began ferrying people again, and Father Kleinsorge asked the theological student to go

across and make his way out to the Jesuit Novitiate at Nagatsuka, about three miles from the center of town, and to request
the priests there to come with help for Fathers Schiffer and
LaSalle. The student got into Mr. Tanimoto's boat and went
off with him. Father Kleinsorge asked Mrs. Nakamura if she
would like to go out to Nagatsuka with the priests when they
came. She said she had some luggage and her children were
sick—they were still vomiting from time to time, and so, for
that matter, was she—and therefore she feared she could not.
He said he thought the fathers from the Novitiate could come
back the next day with a pushcart to get her.

Late in the afternoon, when he went ashore for a while, Mr.
Tanimoto, upon whose energy and initiative many had come
to depend, heard people begging for food. He consulted Father
Kleinsorge, and they decided to go back into town to get some
rice from Mr. Tanimoto's Neighborhood Association shelter
and from the mission shelter. Father Cieslik and two or three
others went with them. At first, when they got among the rows
of prostrate houses, they did not know where they were; the
change was too sudden, from a busy city of two hundred and
forty-five thousand that morning to a mere pattern of residue
in the afternoon. The asphalt of the streets was still so soft and
hot from the fires that walking was uncomfortable. They en-
countered only one person, a woman, who said to them as they
passed, "My husband is in those ashes." At the mission, where
Mr. Tanimoto left the party, Father Kleinsorge was dismayed to
see the building razed. In the garden, on the way to the shelter,
he noticed a pumpkin roasted on the vine. He and Father Cieslik tasted it and it was good. They were surprised at their
hunger, and they ate quite a bit. They got out several bags of
rice and gathered up several other cooked pumpkins and dug
up some potatoes that were nicely baked under the ground, and
started back. Mr. Tanimoto rejoined them on the way. One of
the people with him had some cooking utensils. In the park,
Mr. Tanimoto organized the lightly wounded women of his
neighborhood to cook. Father Kleinsorge offered the Nakamura family some pumpkin, and they tried it, but they could

not keep it on their stomachs. Altogether, the rice was enough to feed nearly a hundred people.

Not All Wounds Were Physical

Just before dark, Mr. Tanimoto came across a twenty-year-old girl, Mrs. Kamai, the Tanimotos' next-door neighbor. She was crouching on the ground with the body of her infant daughter in her arms. The baby had evidently been dead all day. Mrs. Kamai jumped up when she saw Mr. Tanimoto and said, "Would you please try to locate my husband?"

Mr. Tanimoto knew that her husband had been inducted into the Army just the day before; he and Mrs. Tanimoto had entertained Mrs. Kamai in the afternoon, to make her forget. Kamai had reported to the Chugoku Regional Army Headquarters—near the ancient castle in the middle of town—where some four thousand troops were stationed. Judging by the many maimed soldiers Mr. Tanimoto had seen during the day, he surmised that the barracks had been badly damaged by whatever it was that had hit Hiroshima. He knew he hadn't a chance of finding Mrs. Kamai's husband, even if he searched, but he wanted to humor her. "I'll try," he said.

"You've got to find him," she said. "He loved our baby so much. I want him to see her once more."

CHAPTER 2

THE MOVEMENT AND THE NUCLEAR ARMS RACE

AMERICAN
SOCIAL
MOVEMENTS

Organizing a Movement: The First Step Is Arms Control

Leo Szilard

As a scientist working on the Manhattan Project at the University of Chicago, Leo Szilard worked to unite scientists concerned with harnessing atomic power. He coauthored the 1945 Franck Report, in which he and several other project scientists argued against the atomic bombing of Japan and urged the U.S. government to consider the creation of an international panel to oversee all nuclear developments in an effort to avoid a postwar arms race. Both their objections and suggestions went unheeded, and an arms race ensued between the United States and the Soviet Union.

In 1961 Szilard moved to Washington, D.C., in an effort to persuade policymakers to work toward nuclear arms control. However, rather than directly approach the Kennedy administration, Szilard realized that gaining the public's support would be more influential to elected officials. Therefore, in the following speech, delivered in 1961 at Harvard Law School, Szilard proposes the creation of a council of distinguished scientists working in concert with the public to develop and propose nuclear arms control policies, with their ultimate goal being the abolition of all weapons and thus war itself.

The Council for Abolishing War became a reality within a year of Szilard's speech and eventually evolved into the Council for a Livable World—an arms control and disarmament group—that continues to be a presence in the antinuclear movement today.

In Washington, my friends told me that the Government was going to make a sincere effort to reach an agreement with

Excerpted from "Are We on the Road to War?" by Leo Szilard, www.law.harvard.edu, November 17, 1961. Copyright © 1961 by Leo Szilard. Reprinted with permission.

Russia on the cessation of bomb tests and that a reasonable proposal would be made to the Russians on this issue. They would have liked to hear from me that Russia would be likely to accept such a proposal, but coming fresh from Moscow, I had serious doubts on this score.

The Cuban invasion [of 1961] took me by surprise. When I first heard about it, it was not clear, as yet, whether we were going to give air support to the invading Cuban exiles and whether we would, if necessary, send in the Marines also. My immediate reaction was that of alarm, for I believed that if we did any of these things, we would seriously risk war with Russia. I did not think that Russia would try to intervene in the Caribbean area. Nor did I think that the Russians would launch long-range rockets aimed at our cities. I thought, however, that Russia would make some military move elsewhere, perhaps in the Middle East.

In retrospect, it would seem that I was wrong, for Tom Slick [a businessman and philanthropist] of San Antonio, Texas recently disclosed, apparently on good authority, that, if America had openly intervened in Cuba at that point, Russia would have moved into West Berlin.

I would not venture to appraise just how close we came to an all-out war on the occasion of the Cuban incident. I am reasonably certain, however, that if our intervention in Cuba had been successful this would have blocked for many years to come any possibility of reaching an agreement on arms control with Russia. Failure to reach an accommodation on the Berlin issue might, of course, produce the same result.

TRYING TO REACH A COMPROMISE

I would not entirely exclude the possibility of war over Berlin, but, to me, it seems more probable that this crisis will be resolved by some uneasy compromise, and that it will not lead to an all-out war. Russia may bring pressure on West Berlin, in order to promote any one of a number of her foreign policy objectives, but, on the larger issue, the issue of Germany, the true interest of America and Russia is the same. The true interest of both is to have Europe politically as stable as possible.

Neither Russia nor America really knows how to accomplish this goal. America may favor certain solutions and Russia may favor certain other solutions; still, it would be rather odd if America and Russia went to war with each other over the issue of what is the best solution for securing the peace in Europe.

I am convinced that the Berlin issue could be satisfactorily resolved by negotiations, but this conviction is based on the belief that there is something that the Russians want that we should be willing to give them, and that there is something that we want that the Russians should be willing to give us in return.

NATIONAL BIAS INTERVENES

There are many people who do not share this belief. They hold that the Berlin issue was artificially created by Russia for the purpose of humiliating America, for breaking up NATO [the North Atlantic Treaty Organization], and for converting West Germany into a Communist state.

Many people, probably the majority, believe that the Russians are very much like the Nazis; that they have concrete plans for bringing about, one way or another, our total defeat in Europe, and also for subjugating the whole world to their rule.

Many people have a black and white picture of the world; they believe that the nations fall into two classes: the peace-loving nations; and those who are not peace-loving. America, France and England, and generally speaking our allies, including Germany and Japan, are peace-loving nations. Russia and China are not peace-loving nations. Twenty years ago, the situation was somewhat different; at that time, Russia was a peace-loving nation, but Germany and Japan were not.

Many people believe that Russia, by supplying arms on a vast scale to the Chinese Communists, managed to take control of China. They recollect, further, that when American troops fighting [in the Korean War] under the flag of the United Nations, crossed the 38th parallel, moved up across North Korea to the Yalu River, and destroyed the hydro-electric power plant which supplied Manchuria with electricity, all at once—and without any provocation—Chinese Communist hordes crossed the Yalu River and thus frustrated the efforts of the United Nations to unify Korea under free elections.

Many people believe that ever since the atomic bomb forced the unconditional surrender of Japan, America has unceasingly tried to rid the world of the bomb, but that all her efforts were frustrated by Russian intransigence.

PLACING EVENTS IN HISTORICAL PERSPECTIVE

When I listen to people who hold such views, I sometimes have the feeling that I have lived through all this before and, in a sense, I have. I was sixteen years old when the first World War broke out, and I lived at that time in Hungary. From reading the newspapers in Hungary, it would have appeared that, whatever Austria and Germany did was right and whatever England, France, Russia, or America did was wrong. A good case could be made out for this general thesis, in almost every single instance. It would have been difficult for me to prove, in any single instance, that the newspapers were wrong, but somehow, it seemed to me unlikely that the two nations located in the center of Europe should be invariably right, and that all the other nations should be invariably wrong. History, I reasoned, would hardly operate in such a peculiar fashion, and it didn't take long until I began to hold views which were diametrically opposed to those held by the majority of my schoolmates.

Many of my schoolmates regarded me as something of an oracle because I was able to cope with the mysteries of lower arithmetics which baffled them; some of them asked me one day quite early in the war who would lose the war. I said that I didn't know who would lose the war, but that I thought that I knew who ought to lose the war, I thought that Austria and Germany, as well as Russia, ought to lose the war. Since Austria and Germany fought on one side and Russia on the other side, it was not quite clear how this could happen. The fact is, of course, that it did happen.

I am not telling you this in order to impress you with how bright I am. Nobody at sixty can claim to be as bright as he was at sixteen, even though in most cases it is not the intelligence that deteriorates, but the character. The point I am trying to make is that even in times of war, you can see current events in their historical perspective, provided that your passion for the truth prevails over your bias in favor of your own nation.

BIAS PREVAILS

After the war, when I lived in Berlin, a distinguished friend of mine, Michael Polanyi, asked me one day what I thought ought to be the rule of human conduct regulating the behavior of an individual in society. "Clearly," he said, "you cannot simply ask a man to be generous to other people, for if the other people are mean to him, and if he follows your rule, he will starve to death." "But," said Polanyi, "perhaps the rule ought to be 'Be 1 percent more generous to people than they are to you.'" This should be sufficient, he thought, because if everyone were to follow this rule, the earth would, step by step, turn into a livable place.

I told him that, to my mind, this would not work at all, because if two people behave the same way toward each other, each is bound to think that he is 30 percent more generous than the other. Clearly, the rule would have to allow for this bias. Perhaps if we were to stipulate as the rule of conduct, "Be 31 percent more generous to the others than they are to you," such a rule might work.

America and Russia are not following any such rule of conduct. Moreover, their bias greatly exceeds 30 percent. Most Americans apply a yardstick to America's actions which is very different from the yardstick which they apply to Russia's actions. Whenever their bias in favor of their own nation gets into conflict with the truth, the odds are that the bias will prevail. As a result of this, they are not capable of seeing current events in their historical perspective. They may well realize that we are in trouble, but they cannot correctly diagnose the cause of the trouble and therefore, they are not in a position to indicate what the right remedy might be.

WISDOM SUFFERS

The people who have sufficient passion for the truth to give the truth a chance to prevail, if it runs counter to their bias, are in a minority. How important is this "minority?" It is difficult to say at this point, for, at the present time their influence on governmental decisions is not perceptible.

If you stay in Washington, you may gain some insight into the manner in which important governmental decisions come about; you may get a feel of what kind of considerations enter into such decisions, and what kind of pressures are at work.

With President Kennedy, new men moved into the Administration. Many of them fully understand the implications of what is going on and are deeply concerned. But, they are so busy trying to keep the worst things from happening, on a day-to-day basis, that they have no time to develop a consensus on what the right approach would be, from the long-term point of view.

There are also a number of men in Congress, particularly in the Senate, who have insight into what is going on and who are deeply concerned, but they lack the courage of their convictions. They may give a lucid analysis of the trouble in private conversations and then at some point or another, they will say: "Of course, I could not say this in public."

In Washington, wisdom has no chance to prevail at this point. . . .

MUTUAL ASSURED DESTRUCTION

If we intend to drop our bombs on Russia in case of war and expect Russia to drop her bombs on us, so that both countries would be wholly devastated, then our threat to drop bombs on Russia is tantamount to a threat of murder and suicide.

The threat of murder and suicide is not a believable threat, in the context of the Berlin conflict, and it would not be a believable threat in the context of any other similar conflict.

The threat of dropping bombs on Russia, in case of war, would be a believable threat however if America's strategic striking forces were able to cripple most, if not all, of Russia's rocket and bomber bases by one sudden single blow, and if it were America's intention to "strike first" in case of war.

Opinions differ on how successful such a first strike against bases would be today, and whether the Russian counterblow would demolish twenty, ten, one, or none of our cities.

Be that as it may, the Administration will have to decide whether the strategic striking forces of America shall be maintained in the long run at a level where they would have an adequate first strike capability, and whether America should adapt a "first strike against bases if necessary" policy.

The Feasibility of a First-Strike Policy

Let us pause for a moment to examine what such a policy would involve. It would involve, first of all, a great increase in the projected number of solid fuel long-range rockets, and the development of more powerful hydrogen warheads for these rockets. This would be necessary because the Russians would, of course, harden their rocket bases.

Secondly, it would involve the manufacture of a large number of rockets that would function as decoys, in order to neutralize the anti-missile missiles, by means of which the Russians may be expected to defend their rocket bases.

Further, since we could not expect to destroy every single Russian base and submarine in a first strike, we would have to embark on a major development program in order to have adequate anti-missile missiles available for the defense of our cities.

And lastly, we would be more or less forced to embark on a shelter program involving an annual expenditure of perhaps $20 billion. The shelters would have to protect not only against fall-out, but also against heat and blast. The problem of getting the people into the shelters at the right time would probably offer no major obstacle, since if we plan to strike first, the

Government should be in a position to get the people to take shelter at the right time.

Only if such defensive measures were included in the program would the maintenance of a first strike against bases capability permit America to retain the bomb as a deterrent.

To me it seems conceivable that America's strategic striking force could be boosted to the level where, for a limited period of time, they would be capable of an adequate first strike against bases. It is not likely, however, that they could be maintained indefinitely at such a level. Presumably periods when America has a first strike capability would alternate with periods when she does not have such a capability. And if there were a major international crisis during one of the periods when we have a first strike capability, the Government would be under strong pressure to start a preventive war.

The decision to start a preventive war would always be a hard decision for any President to take, particularly since he would never be quite certain just how many of our own cities would be hit. But in certain circumstances, his hand could be forced by a commander of an overseas strategic base, or a submarine capable of launching rockets.

If a commander of a strategic base or a submarine were to drop bombs on, say, three Russian cities, then the Russians would be expected to strike back with all they have, and the President would have no choice but to order an all-out first strike against the bases of Russians.

A "first strike if necessary" policy would mean an atomic arms race, with the sky as the limit. I do not believe that America could be made secure by trying to keep ahead in such an arms race, and I would be in favor of resisting the adoption of such a policy, if necessary through vigorous political action.

WORKING TOWARD NUCLEAR ARMS CONTROL

In deciding against such a policy, we must, however, recognize, that if America renounces the "first strike if necessary" policy, she loses the deterrent effect of her strategic striking forces. For, clearly, if these forces are not capable of a first strike against Russian bases, then any threat that America would attack Russia with bombs, in case of war, would be tantamount to a threat of murder and suicide and would, therefore, not be believable.

If America renounces the first strike policy, then the strategic striking forces of America could thereafter function only as protection. If these forces are arranged in such a manner that a sudden attack on them could not substantially reduce their ability to strike a major counter-blow, then these forces may be looked upon as protection against the possibility that America might be attacked with bombs.

A clear policy decision to the effect that America is going to maintain an invulnerable second strike but would not adopt a "first strike if necessary" policy would leave open the door to an agreement on arms control. This is important, because an agreement on arms control (providing for far-reaching disarmament) is a necessary first step towards abolishing war.

An agreement on arms control would have to involve, however, not only Russia but also China, and it is not likely that negotiations including China may get under way within the next twelve months. It might very well be, therefore, that in the immediate future America would have to take unilateral steps in order to reduce the present danger of an all-out war. . . .

I believe that, at the present time, little could be gained by bringing pressure on the Administration to enter into formal negotiations with Russia on the issue of General Disarmament, because—as they say, "You can lead a horse to the water, but you can't make him drink."

I believe that no substantial progress will be made towards disarmament until Americans and Russians first reach a meeting of the minds on the issue of how the peace may be secured in a disarmed world. . . .

I would ask seven to twelve distinguished scientists to form a Council, which might be called the Council for Abolishing War or perhaps better, Council for a Livable World. This Council would, first of all, assemble a panel of political advisers, whose identity would be public knowledge and formulate in close consultations with those advisers two sets of objectives. To the first set belong those objectives which cannot be attained at the present time through political action because it would take further inquiry, and perhaps even research, to know, in concrete terms, what needs to be done. To the second set belong those objectives which can be pursued through political action, because it is clear what needs to be done.

The members of the Council would set up a Research Organization aimed at the pursuit of the first set of objectives, and they would serve as the Trustees of that organization.

The members of the Council would also set up a political organization aimed at the pursuit of the second set of objectives, and they would serve as the Board of Directors for that organization. Because one of the functions of the second organization would be to pursue political objectives we may refer to it . . . as "The Lobby".

It seems to me that there is no need to create a membership organization and to enlist those who are interested as members of such an organization. What one needs to create is not a membership organization, but a Movement.

The Kennedy-Hatfield Resolution for a Nuclear Freeze

EDWARD M. KENNEDY

Edward M. Kennedy, the Democratic senator from Massachusetts since 1962, is still acknowledged as a leader of Senate liberals today. On becoming a member of the Senate Armed Services Committee in 1983, he opposed the untested "Star Wars" program (which advocated developing a space-based ballistic missile defense system), publicly showing his support for nuclear arms control. Almost twenty years later, Senator Kennedy found himself once again opposing a Star Wars–like program: President George W. Bush's national missile defense system.

On March 10, 1982, along with Republican senator Mark O. Hatfield, Kennedy introduced a U.S. Senate resolution calling for a freeze on the testing, production, and further deployment of nuclear warheads, missiles, and other delivery systems within the United States and the Soviet Union. Kennedy and Hatfield also proposed that a significant reduction follow the freeze. Their resolution helped the freeze movement reach its peak during the 1980s. By the end of 1982, voters in eight states passed referenda calling for a mutual and verifiable freeze on the testing, production, and deployment of nuclear weapons, and by the mid-1980s, Catholic, Protestant, and Jewish leaders voiced their support as well. At the end of the decade, nearly seventy-five arms control groups came together to form the U.S. Comprehensive Test Ban Coalition, known today as the Coalition to Reduce Nuclear Dangers.

In the following selection, Kennedy places his resolution within the sociopolitical context of 1982. Despite the resolution having

Excerpted from Edward M. Kennedy's testimony before the Senate Committee on Foreign Relations, May 11, 1982.

twenty-six cosponsors and a hearing before the Committee on Foreign Relations, no action was ever taken on this resolution. Rather than "pursue a complete halt to the nuclear arms race," as Senators Kennedy and Hatfield urged, the committee replaced their resolution with one introduced by former Illinois Republican senator Charles H. Percy, which states in more hesitant language that instead of an immediate freeze, both the United States and the Soviet Union should work toward reduction if possible.

O ur proposal calls for a mutual and verifiable freeze on the testing, production, and further deployment of nuclear warheads, missiles and other delivery systems with the Soviet Union, followed by major stabilizing reductions in the nuclear arsenals on both sides.

We recognize the distance that the [Ronald] Reagan Administration has come on this issue in recent weeks and months [in 1982]. We welcome the President's new and more affirmative attitude towards arms control. The Administration's movement on this issue is a tribute to the growing effectiveness of another movement of great importance—the nationwide grassroots campaign to stop the nuclear arms race by achieving a nuclear weapons freeze.

The prevention of nuclear war is not only the great issue of our time, but perhaps the greatest issue of all time. Today the two superpowers possess the equivalent of one million Hiroshima bombs—an amount equal to four tons of T.N.T. for every man, woman, and child presently living on this planet.

Like building blocks stacked one upon the other in a child's playroom, the nuclear weapons buildup has lifted all of us to higher and higher levels of danger. Inexorably, we are moving toward the point where the slightest accident or miscalculation could bring the whole structure tumbling down, and plunge our two nations and the world into nuclear holocaust. The Kennedy-Hatfield Resolution insists that we must stop the nuclear buildup now, before we reach the point of nuclear no return.

The President has now spoken about the need to restrain

nuclear arms. But my basic concern over the President's plan is that his START [Strategic Arms Reduction Talks] proposal does not stop the nuclear arms race; it merely channels it into a new direction. It permits the continued testing, production, and deployment of the MX missile, the Trident II missile, the Cruise missile, the B-1 bomber, the Stealth bomber, and other advanced nuclear weapons. Indeed, the Reagan plan does not cover bombers or Cruise missiles at all—a loophole big enough to fly a fleet of bombers through, with each plane carrying more destructive force than all the bombs dropped in World War II.

While the United States builds more, the Soviet Union will not be standing idle. They have their own new weapons on their own drawing boards—including the Typhoon submarine and a follow-on generation of missiles beyond the current SS-18s and SS-19s.

As recent history demonstrates, the Soviets are prepared to match us every step and every missile of the way in the futile but increasingly dangerous quest for nuclear superiority. You do not have to be an Isaac Newton to understand the first law of the nuclear arms race—every action by one side will be matched by an equal and opposite reaction by the other side.

I believe that a nuclear weapons freeze is the most effective way to halt the nuclear arms race now, so that we can finally begin to run it in reverse. The fundamental question which I ask is the fundamental question that citizens in communities across the country are asking in ever-increasing numbers: Mr. President, why not start with a freeze as the first step toward arms control?

We do not enter a freeze or reduction of nuclear arms because we like the Soviets or they like us—but because both of us prefer existence to extinction.

A Mutual Freeze Will Lead to Mutual Reductions

A nuclear weapons freeze has the clear advantage of bypassing endless, irresolvable arguments about which side is ahead.

U.S. Catholic Bishops Support Weapons Freeze and Disarmament

1. We support immediate, bilateral, verifiable agreements to halt the testing, production and deployment of new nuclear weapons systems. This recommendation is not to be identified with any specific political initiative.

2. We support efforts to achieve deep cuts in the arsenals of both superpowers; efforts should concentrate first on systems which threaten the retaliatory forces of either major power.

3. We support early and successful conclusion of negotiations of a comprehensive test ban treaty.

4. We urge new efforts to prevent the spread of nuclear weapons in the world and to control the conventional arms race, particularly the conventional arms trade.

5. We support in an increasingly interdependent world political and economic policies designed to protect human dignity and to promote the human rights of every person, especially the least among us. In this regard we call for the establishment of some form of global authority adequate to the needs of the international common good.

Official summary of U.S. Bishops' 1983 pastoral letter.

Too often, we find that equality is in the eye of the beholder. In fact, both sides today are at essential parity. Each side, even after absorbing a first strike, can destroy the other many times over. The United States can make the Soviet rubble bounce all the way from Moscow to Vladivostok, and the Soviets can make our rubble bounce all the way from the Potomac to the Pacific. The Kennedy-Hatfield Resolution accepts this condition of parity; it calls for a mutual freeze now, with mutual reductions to follow, in the interest of preventing mutual annihilation.

At best, the Administration must anticipate protracted negotiations with the Soviets over any such proposal. Now, in this posture, a nuclear freeze could well make all the difference to the success or failure of the Reagan plan. A freeze is the only idea which can stop the spiral of nuclear arms development in the near term, and avoid the self-defeating delays of long-term negotiations over arms reductions.

A freeze agreement would be a nuclear weapons firebreak. Once armaments and technological advances are stopped at present levels, the two superpowers can negotiate phased and balanced reductions. President Reagan has called for one-third reductions in ballistic missile warheads. The Kennedy-Hatfield Resolution calls for across-the-board reductions "through annual percentages or equally effective means." George Kennan, our former ambassador to the Soviet Union and our foremost expert on that country, and Admiral Hyman G. Rickover, Director of Naval Nuclear Propulsion under seven presidents, have argued eloquently and compellingly for deep cuts of at least 50 percent in the nuclear armories of both sides. These cuts could be achieved by the end of this decade if we mutually agree to reasonable reductions of seven percent a year. This is the approach proposed in the Kennedy-Hatfield Resolution.

A FREEZE WILL END THE ARMS RACE

Finally, a freeze will enhance, not reduce, our overall national security. It will halt the development of more powerful Soviet rockets and block their further deployment of existing weapons. It will prevent one side from perfecting its capacity for a first strike against the other by prohibiting the testing and production of such destabilizing weapons; the result will be a substantial reduction in the fear of a U.S. or Soviet pre-emptive attack. And a freeze will also permit additional resources to be allocated to our conventional military forces, where we do need to do more.

Opponents of a freeze claim that the Soviets would have no incentive to reduce their arsenals after a freeze. They call for building new weapons systems, in order to pile up bargaining chips for later negotiations with the Kremlin.

The arms race has been needlessly and heedlessly perpetuated by this bargaining chip theory, because both sides inevitably feel forced to match new and threatening developments with their own. A decade ago, MIRVs [multiple independently targetable reentry vehicles] were defended as a bargaining chip during the SALT [Strategic Arms Limitation Talks] I talks. The United States continued to deploy them, and then we were told that they were too important to bargain away.

ONLY THREE STEPS TO ARMS CONTROL

The Administration says that it wants to go beyond a freeze and do better. But with $100 billion worth of new weapons now in prospect over the next five years, the Administration is still far short of a freeze. I believe the best arms control approach is not to brandish an arms race as a means of achieving arms reduction, but a combination of three important steps:

First, the Administration should pledge unequivocally that it will abide by the limits of the SALT II Treaty, so long as the Soviets also do. The President has been unwilling to give such a pledge thus far.

Second, in order to prevent massive build-ups on either side during prolonged negotiations for reductions, the Administration should propose to the Soviet Union a mutual and verifiable nuclear weapons freeze.

Third, the Administration should seek to negotiate major reductions in all aspects of nuclear forces, not simply in one or two elements of those forces.

Past arms control agreements have been defective, because they have failed to prevent quantum leaps in the sophistication of weaponry. The Vladivostok accord and the SALT II Treaty permitted the development of cruise missiles. The military planners saw the loophole and decided to rush through it with a new weapons system in which they had previously shown only minimum interest.

ADHERENCE TO A FREEZE CAN BE VERIFIED

Where there is a loophole, it will almost certainly be exploited. Where a new system is permitted, it will inevitably be pursued, in order to prevent the adversary from gaining an advantage. A comprehensive freeze, put in place before reductions talks begin, will plug past loopholes and prevent future ones by blocking any further additions to current nuclear arsenals.

Opponents of a nuclear weapons freeze also claim that a freeze is not a practical idea, because it will be difficult to verify. I believe that just the opposite is true. In fact, a freeze may well be easier to verify than a complex arms reduction agreement.

In a matter of months, the two superpowers, assuming their goodwill, could reasonably work out satisfactory verification procedures for a freeze. Members of the Reagan Administration, supporters of the Jackson-Warner Resolution, and other critics of the Kennedy-Hatfield Resolution who claim that a freeze is unverifiable are exhibiting a surprising inconsistency in their logic—they say they will support a freeze tomorrow, after we build some more today. So they too must believe that a freeze actually can be verified.

In fact, the Kennedy-Hatfield Resolution does not require trust by one side for the other. Every element of the freeze depends on strict verification. What cannot be verified will not be frozen. But there are many experts who agree that a freeze is adequately verifiable.

It may be that some form of on-site inspection will be necessary to verify production and to check certain limited aspects of testing. To presume that the Soviets will not permit any such inspection overlooks the record of the comprehensive test-ban treaty negotiations, now postponed by the Reagan Administration, where the Soviets have agreed to the principle of on-site verification. Even areas where there may be verification questions, such as some areas of production, do not present serious difficulties, since verification in other areas will assure overall enforcement of the freeze.

NOTHING SHORT OF A GLOBAL FREEZE

Critics of the freeze sometimes confuse it with the Soviet proposal for a European freeze. The Kennedy-Hatfield Resolution rejects a freeze in Europe alone. Our proposal is for a global freeze. In case of a Soviet nuclear attack on NATO [the North Atlantic Treaty Organization], the United States could call on its entire nuclear arsenal to respond. For any Administration to suggest that it no longer relies on this option would signal a major and destabilizing change in NATO policy, in which Europe would no longer enjoy the protection of America's nuclear umbrella.

On the critical issue of ending the nuclear arms race now and reducing the arsenals of nuclear annihilation, I believe the Kennedy-Hatfield Resolution provides a vital alternative, and I urge the committee to approve it. Whether we prevail at first or not in this cause, and no matter how long it may take, I will continue to stand, to speak and to work for a nuclear weapons freeze—and so will millions of citizens in every section of the country. The American people want to stop the arms race before it stops the human race.

Why Abolish Nuclear Weapons?

NUCLEAR AGE PEACE FOUNDATION

The Nuclear Age Peace Foundation works to eliminate the nuclear weapons threat to humanity and to build a legacy of peace through education and advocacy. The following brief, issued in 1998, outlines the six reasons why abolishing nuclear weapons is an achievable goal.

The foundation not only cites the illegality and immorality of using nuclear weapons but also the costliness of their production and maintenance. Because the existence of nuclear arsenals has not deterred military conflicts, and because several nations have become nuclear weapons–free states without compromising their security, the foundation urges the United States to embrace the words of former secretary of defense William Perry: "Sunflowers instead of missiles in the soil would insure peace for future generations."

*R*eason One: The entire world would be more secure if the planet were free of nuclear weapons.

Nuclear weapons are the only type of weapon in existence that have the capacity to annihilate the human species and countless other species.

The very existence of nuclear weapons leaves open the possibility that a nuclear exchange might take place. This could happen intentionally, inadvertently (as in the [1962] Cuban Missile Crisis when the U.S. and USSR almost blundered into nuclear war), or by an accidental launch. The list of historical false alarms is long; for instance, in 1979 someone fed a war game simulation into a North American Air Defense computer. Thinking that the alert was real, fighter planes were scrambled and nuclear bombers were readied before the error was discovered.

In the absence of total nuclear disarmament, terrorists might acquire nuclear weapons. Such a scenario has become more probable since the USSR dissolved. There have been many reports of attempts to smuggle weapons-grade plutonium from Russia. The fewer nuclear weapons there are in the world, the fewer there are for terrorists to try to steal. Every step toward the abolition of nuclear weapons would increase our security.

Without abolition, there is always the danger that nuclear weapons will proliferate—that more and more countries will obtain them. It is ultimately unrealistic to expect that in a world in which some nations rely upon nuclear weapons, other nations will not seek to attain them. A world where there are many nuclear-armed countries would be even more dangerous.

The end of the Cold War has meant that there are no more nuclear-armed opponents, except India and Pakistan. Nuclear weapons do not serve even an arguable purpose when a country has friendly relations with a former opponent.

Reason Two: The threat or use of nuclear weapons has been declared generally illegal by the World Court.

The July 8, 1996 decision of the International Court of Justice stated that it is generally illegal to use or to threaten to use nuclear weapons. From a legal point of view, it would be virtually impossible to use nuclear weapons without violating the laws of armed conflict. The International Security and Arms Control Committee of the U.S. National Academy of Sciences concluded that "the inherent destructiveness of nuclear weapons, combined with the unavoidable risk that even the most restricted use of such weapons would escalate to broader attacks, makes it extremely unlikely that any contemplated threat or use of nuclear weapons would meet these [the Court's] criteria." If nuclear armed nations are serious about upholding international law, they ought to immediately commence negotiations for eliminating and prohibiting all nuclear weapons.

Reason Three: Nuclear weapons are morally reprehensible.

The rightness of many issues is debatable, but nuclear weapons are morally insupportable. Even possessing something so deadly is wrong. These radiation-laden bombs can destroy most life on Earth and would be better described as national and global suicide devices rather than weapons. What could be more evil? As Joseph Rotblat, the 1995 Nobel Peace Laureate, urged when speaking against nuclear weapons, "Remember your humanity!"

Father Richard McSorley has written, "Can we go along with the intent to use nuclear weapons? What it is wrong to do, it is wrong to intend to do. If it is wrong for me to kill you, it is wrong for me to plan to do it. If I get my gun and go into your house to retaliate for a wrong done me, then find there are police guarding your house, I have already committed murder in my heart. I have intended it. *Likewise, if I intend to use nuclear weapons in massive retaliation, I have already committed massive murder in my heart.*" (emphasis added)

Such intentions to harm violate the moral teachings of all religions. It is worth remembering that even in the middle of a war as bitterly fought as World War II, some generals and admirals opposed the use of the first nuclear weapons on the grounds that it was immoral to kill civilians. Their moral arguments are truer today than when first uttered, since a war with current, superpowerful H-bombs [hydrogen bombs] would poison entire continents. What kind of people do we become, if we accept the possibility of committing mass murder and suicide as part of our everyday government policy?

Reason Four: Nuclear weapons have not prevented wars, which is what they were supposed to do.

Nuclear weapons certainly have NOT prevented wars between nuclear weapons states and non–nuclear weapons states. (Ask any Vietnam or Gulf War veteran!) Nuclear weapons states have been involved in more wars than non–nuclear weapons states. Between 1945 and 1997, nuclear weapons states have fought in an average of 5.2 wars, while non–nuclear weapons states averaged about 0.67 wars.

Some advocates of nuclear weapons continue to claim that such weapons have at least prevented a large-scale conflict between major powers (specifically between the U.S. and the former USSR). Though there have not been any world wars since the development and use of nuclear weapons, this is not proof that nuclear weapons have been responsible for keeping the peace. It is unclear that any of the major powers wanted to fight on a large scale with each other.

According to the [1996] Canberra Commission on the Elimination of Nuclear Weapons, the idea that the former Soviet Union was plotting to invade Europe is open to question in light of recent investigations made possible due to the end of the Cold War. The horrific experiences of World War II, in which some 40 to 50 million people died, had convinced leaders in both the East and the West that another world war should be avoided at almost any price.

Some even claim that the presence of nuclear weapons in war-prone regions such as India and Pakistan has introduced caution and served as a stabilizing force. Others suggest, however, that Pakistan's acquisition of a nuclear capability has hardened its resolve not to settle the Kashmir crisis and allowed it to feel safe behind a "nuclear shield" as it supports Kashmiri militancy.

If the only use of nuclear weapons is to deter enemy use of nuclear weapons, then the best way to end the threat of nuclear war is to eliminate these weapons altogether.

Reason Five: Nuclear weapons are extraordinarily costly, and the costs continue into the indefinite future.

Although nuclear weapons were promoted in the 1950s with the idea that they would provide "more bang for the buck," just the opposite is true. When the costs of research, development, testing, deployment, maintenance and associated intelligence activities are combined, the price tag is hefty. When costs of damage to the land, illnesses of uranium miners, cancer deaths from nuclear pollution, and storage of nuclear waste for centuries are added, the price becomes astronomical. Since the early 1940s, the U.S. alone has spent over

$4 trillion ($4,000,000,000,000) on nuclear arms. Note that this is the approximate size of the U.S. national debt! (No one knows how much it will cost to clean up leaking waste sites now and store weapons-related nuclear wastes for many thousands of years.)

If current policies are implemented, the U.S. will continue to spend some $25–$30 billion per year on its nuclear forces. Consider the fact that the U.S. government has allocated $27 billion for education, and $17 billion for housing assistance for 1997. What is more important—educational assistance or bombs that can incinerate millions of people? As we consider the cost of nuclear weapons, we should also keep in mind that one in seven individuals in the U.S. lives below the poverty line, and some 30 million U.S. citizens are without adequate medical insurance. We have lots better things to spend our tax dollars on than gigantic weapons that are not related to any realistic estimate of our military needs.

Reason Six: Some countries have already given up nuclear weapons, showing that it is possible for a nation to be secure without them.

Three former Soviet republics, Belarus, Kazakhstan and Ukraine, became nuclear weapons free states by voluntarily transferring their nuclear warheads to Russia after the breakup of the Soviet Union. South Africa actually developed a small nuclear arsenal clandestinely, and then dismantled it. Argentina and Brazil have also eliminated their nuclear weapons programs even though they achieved initial success in these programs.

On June 4, 1996, the U.S. Secretary of Defense met with the defense ministers of Russia and Ukraine to celebrate Ukraine's change in status from the world's third largest nuclear weapons state to a nuclear weapon free state. On the occasion, these defense leaders planted sunflowers and scattered sunflower seeds on a former Ukrainian missile base that once housed eighty SS-19 missiles aimed at the United States. U.S. Secretary of Defense William Perry said, "Sunflowers instead of missiles in the soil would insure peace for future generations."

Nuclear Weapons Abolition: The Major Issues

JOHN M. LAFORGE

John M. LaForge is codirector of Nukewatch, a peace and environmental action group that focuses on the nuclear industry, and editor of its newsletter, the *Pathfinder*. The group advocates nonviolent action and public education to achieve the abolition of all nuclear weapons.

Pointing out that peace and antinuclear organizations have been joined by scientific panels, retired and eminent military officials, and nuclear weapons designers in the fight against nuclear proliferation, LaForge has faith in the power of the current movement to influence U.S. policy. In the following selection he outlines the crucial issues concerning nuclear weapons abolition: denouncing first use of nuclear weapons as well as strikes against nonnuclear states, disclosing all secret military programs, and admitting that the main reason for continuing the production of nuclear weapons—to avoid war and the further loss of life—is self-deluding propaganda.

Only by urging the United States to move forward—only by refusing to take "no" for an answer—will the movement achieve victory on the road to nuclear weapons abolition.

The clamor for nuclear disarmament is being raised by millions the world over not only by established peace and anti-nuclear organizations, but by NGOs [nongovernmental organizations], scientific panels, retired generals, eminent military and civilian officials, nuclear weapons designers, and international judges. With the influential weight of these new

Excerpted from "Nuclear Politics—Nuclear Disarmament: Hiroshima's and Nagasaki's Lessons Still to Be Learned," by John M. LaForge, *Z Magazine,* July/August 1998. Copyright © 1998 by *Z Magazine*. Reprinted with permission.

voices, the United States has an opportunity to reconsider official nuclear weapons policy and to achieve four important victories in route to the bomb's abolition: A pledge of "no first use"; a promise of no use of nuclear weapons against non–nuclear-armed states; a disclosure and accounting of secret military programs; a formal renunciation of the "usefulness" of the bomb.

PLEDGE "NO FIRST USE"

The United States' atomic bombings were the "first use" of nuclear weapons in more ways than one. In modern parlance, nuclear "first use" means the escalation from conventional bombing or the threat of it, to the initiation of nuclear warfare. The U.S. government was not only the first to use nuclear weapons in war but the first to escalate from conventional to nuclear bombardment. The Pentagon still uses the "first use" threat, as in the 1991 Persian Gulf bombing campaign, during which government officials, including Defense Secretary Dick Cheney and Secretary of State James Baker, "continued to publicly hint that the United States might retaliate with nuclear weapons." Following their lead, U.S. Representative Dan Burton (R-IN), syndicated columnist Cal Thomas, and others publicly advocated bombing Iraq with nuclear weapons in the midst of the U.S.-led bombardment.

In April 1996, the [Bill] Clinton administration's Herald Smith publicly threatened to use nuclear weapons against the African state of Libya—a member in good standing of the Nuclear Nonproliferation Treaty—for allegedly building a weapons plant. When then Defense Secretary William Perry was questioned about Smith's threat, he only reiterated it, saying about using U.S. nuclear weapons against non-nuclear Libya, "we would not forswear that possibility." (The nonproliferation treaty forbids any nuclear attack against states that are party to it.)

[In November 1997], the Clinton administration made public in Presidential Policy Directive 60 the "first-use" intentions of its nuclear warfare planners. The announcement was that U.S. H-bombs [hydrogen bombs] are aimed at Third World nations said by the Department of State to be administered by "rogue" governments. "The directive is notable for language that would allow the United States to launch nuclear weapons in response to the use of chemical or biological weapons." The presidential announcement was accompanied by a statement by senior National Security Council staffer Robert Bell who said, "The [Directive] requires a wide range of nuclear retaliatory options, from a limited strike to a more general nuclear exchange." And "Clinton ordered that the military . . . reserve the right to use nuclear arms first, even before the detonation of an enemy warhead."

This newly announced first-strike policy flies in the face of the prestigious National Academy of Sciences (NAS), the nation's highest scientific advisory group, which recommended [in] June [1997] that the United States, "declare that it will not be the first to use nuclear weapons in war or crisis." The Clinton administration seemed to directly dismiss the NAS's advice when, in April 1998, the U.S. Embassy in Moscow flatly refused to rule out the possible use of nuclear warheads against Iraq, saying "we do not rule out in advance any capability available to us."

Pledging "no first use" would save billions of dollars in research and development, as well as the cost of maintenance of systems designed to strike first: the MX, Trident I and II, Cruise and Minuteman III missiles and the B-1 and Stealth bombers. Forswearing nuclear "first use" wouldn't be risky in geopolitical terms because the United States has no nuclear-armed enemies, and all the other nuclear-armed states (Britain, China, France, India, Israel, and Russia) are either allies, "most favored nations," clients, or military Don Quixoties.

Further, a "no first use" pledge would free U.S. presidents from threatening to go nuclear, officially unacknowledged terrorism they have practiced many times. Putting an end to these ultimate bomb threats would bring U.S. actions in line with its current rhetoric: President Clinton denounced "nuclear terrorism" on June 15, 1995, en route to the [economic] summit meeting in Halifax.

Significantly, the nuclear weapons states who have used their first strike "master card" believe they've succeeded with their dreadful risk-taking—the way an extortionist can get what he wants without ever pulling the trigger. Nuclear war planners want to keep this "ace" up their sleeve. Sadly, since official history has it that the U.S. Army Air Corps' atomic bombings of Japan ware justified, there is a heavy stigma against formally renouncing another first use. To do so might seem to call into question the rationale of having crossed the line back then.

PROMISE NO NUCLEAR STRIKES

Using the bomb against non-nuclear Japan followed the mass destruction of Dresden and Hamburg in Germany and the indiscriminate fire bombings of Kobe, Osaka, Yokohama, and Tokyo in Japan. In August 1945, the power disparity between nuclear and "conventional" firestorms must have appeared small. However, the atom bomb's real punch—initially denied and by nature delayed for many years—is now known to be cancer, leukemia, birth defects, and weakened immune system function for generation upon generation. Today's U.S. warheads are from 12 to 96 times the magnitude of the Hiroshima blast: from 150 kiloton (Kt) warheads on Cruise missiles, to the 1,200 Kt (1.2 megaton) B-83 bombs aboard the air force's heavy bombers.

The deadly power of modern H-bombs (more accurately "radiation bombs") gives the demand for a "non-nuclear immunity" pledge the advantage of being fair and rational. The so-called "rogue states" that the U.S. State Department claims want to join the Nuclear Club—Libya, North Korea, Iraq, Iran, Syria, and Cuba—have a combined military budget of $15.3 billion (Libya: $1 billion; N. Korea: $6 billion; Iraq: $3 billion; Iran: $2 billion; Syria: $3 billion; Cuba: $0.3 billion). This is less than one-ninth of the Pentagon's annual $300-plus billion (including NASA, Energy Department, and National Guard). The 1991 Persian Gulf bombardment and the decade-long bombings of Vietnam, Laos, and Cambodia, proved to the non-nuclear states and all the world and should have proved to our own that nuclear weapons are superfluous and totally unnecessary when the government chooses to destroy small countries.

The agreement on non-nuclear immunity made May 11, 1995 by the five declared Nuclear Club members will not quell legitimate charges of hypocrisy made against them. The pact is full of exceptions and is not binding. Only China has made an unequivocal pledge: "At no time and under no circumstances will China be the first to use nuclear weapons and (China) undertakes unconditionally not to use or threaten to use nuclear weapons against non-nuclear countries and nuclear-free zones."

In spite of the possible taint of impropriety that may accrue to the atomic bombings of Japan, the United States should end its opposition to adopting China's unambiguous language and promise never to use nuclear weapons against non-nuclear states.

DISCLOSE SECRET MILITARY PROGRAMS

The building, testing, and unleashing of the bomb in 1945 was done in total secrecy by the Manhattan Project. The Project provided the unprecedented political insurance that was necessary for such extravagant spending on such a dubious program. It might never have "worked." One consequence of the Project's leap into hidden government spending—ironically, all done in the name of combating anti-democratic militarism—is that a militarized and anti-democratic process was institutionalized.

Witness the 4,000 secret radiation experiments conducted under the auspices of the U.S. military against more than 16,000 U.S. civilians: pregnant women, retarded children, prison inmates, cancer patients, the terminally ill, and stolen cadavers. Former Energy Secretary Hazel O'Leary confessed shock about the U.S. scientists' actions. "I said, 'Who were these people [conducting the experiments] and why did this happen?' The only thing I could think of was Nazi Germany." Official misconduct on such a scale could not have occurred without the nuclear establishment's grant of complete secrecy.

If further proof were needed that such official secrecy

breeds more wrong-doing than it prevents, we have hundreds of thousands of tons of military radioactive wastes that have been injected into deep wells, dumped into the water table, buried in shallow trenches, and thrown into the oceans (our nuclear submarines still routinely release "allowable" amounts of liquid and gaseous radioactive wastes into the oceans) that will threaten living things with cancer and reproductive abnormalities forever. The U.S. government's cover-up of these ethical and environmental outrages was exposed in 20 front-page *New York Times* articles in 1989.

The classified Pentagon budget has now ballooned to about $30 billion or more per year. The official secrecy this fund is afforded protects programs and adventures that may not be legal, but, because they're secret, cannot be challenged in Congress, the courts, or the press. Indeed, the secret budget continues to exist because the boondoggles that it keeps secret could not withstand public or Congressional oversight.

One example is the Navy's Project ELF, which for years has been attacked in Congress as a "cold war relic." The ELF [extremely low frequency] transmitter sends one-way orders to submerged, nuclear-armed U.S. and British submarines around the world. This nuclear war "starter pistol" was saved from certain cancellation in April 1995 by a so-called "classified emergency reason" originating with the Navy. The nuclear war fighting function of ELF (along with its potentially harmful non-ionizing electromagnetic radiation) made it an easy target for deficit hawks, so its budget had earlier been cut. The Navy's maneuver—by way of the "secret emergency" which is still unknown to the public—convinced a House-Senate conference committee to restore the funding. U.S. Senator Russ Feingold (D-WI), who has repeatedly sponsored legislation to terminate Project ELF, was unconvinced by what he called an "eleventh-hour trick," saying, "The Navy explicitly told me there was no 'classified' reason for maintaining ELF." Hundreds of these cold war dinosaurs are still being maintained inside secret programs that, if made public, would make laughing stocks of the military contractors—and the taxpayers.

ADMIT THE USELESSNESS OF THE BOMB

Calling nuclear warheads "fundamentally useless," the National Academy of Sciences, in the June 1997 report mentioned earlier, charged that current U.S. nuclear war fighting plans were "largely unchanged from the cold war era" when 30,000 H-bombs were targeted at the former USSR and China. This NAS rejection of the bomb is a far cry from current State Department policy and amounts to a startling condemnation of official U.S. history.

There has for 50 years been a debate about whether the destruction of Hiroshima and Nagasaki was "necessary." Although critical voices have generally been drowned by the soothing official paradox that "the Bomb saved lives," negative answers are not hard to find. In 1945, Brig. Gen. Bonnie Feller wrote, "Neither the atomic bombing nor the entry of the Soviet Union into the war forced Japan's unconditional surrender." Historian Gar Alperovitz (*Atomic Diplomacy,* Penguin Books, 1985 and *The Decision to Use the Atomic Bomb,* Random House, 1996) has said, "I think it can be proven that the bomb was not only unnecessary but known in advance not to be necessary." President Dwight Eisenhower said it wasn't necessary: "First, the Japanese were ready to surrender and it wasn't necessary to hit them with that awful thing. Second, I hated to see our country be the first to use such a weapon."

These charges, as contrary to the government story as they are, share a wrongheaded implication; namely, that nuclear warfare could conceivably be "necessary" or "excusable" under some circumstances. That most people in the United States still believe this to be true is the result of decades of myth-making started by President Truman, who said, "The world will note that the first atomic bomb was dropped on Hiroshima, a military base. That was because we wished this first attack to avoid, insofar as possible, the killing of civilians."

Taking President Truman at his word, the 140,000 civilians killed at Hiroshima are the minimum to be expected when exploding a small nuclear weapon on a "military base." At this rate today's "small" (Cruise missile) warheads, which are 12 times the power of Truman's bomb, might "avoid" killing any more, but would kill a minimum of 1.68 million civilians.

The ability to think of such acts as "necessary"—and to prepare and to threaten them—requires the adoption of a learned indifference that insulates the conscience of the executioner. Such a deep-seated denial is needed in order to excuse any mass destruction because, generally, the rightness of indiscriminate attacks is not debatable whether in Oklahoma City, Sarajevo, Rwanda, or Hiroshima. Furthermore, since the H-bomb can produce only uncontrollable, widespread, and long-term results, it follows that the rationalization of U.S. nuclear war planning has hardly changed since 1945. Consider how similar to President Truman's words (above) are those of the U.S. State Department's recent declaration to the International Court of Justice (the World Court) on the question of the legality of using nuclear weapons: "Nuclear weapons can be directed at a military target and can be used in a discriminate manner."

This artful lie, the engine of the nuclear weapons establishment, amounts to the cynical and outlawed notion that good can come from the commission of mass destruction. The State Department's claim cannot, no matter how often or skillfully repeated, make the effects of even one nuclear warhead limited, controllable, militarily practical or ethically justifiable.

In his October 3, 1996 speech to the State of the World Forum in San Francisco, Gen. George Lee Butler became the first U.S. Strategic Air Command (SAC) commander in history to condemn U.S. nuclear weapons and nuclear war policy, a policy he had molded and implemented, saying in part, "A renewed appreciation for the obscene power of a single nuclear weapon is taking a new hold on our consciousness." He delivered the same statement to the National Press Club December 4, 1996. In a more recent essay, Gen. Butler has said that President Clinton's nuclear war policy is based on the mistaken belief that "nuclear weapons retain an aura of utility." Gen. Butler argues that "Too many of us have failed to properly understand the risks and consequences of nuclear war. [Nuclear weapons'] effects transcend time and place, poisoning the earth and deforming its inhabitants for generation[s]." Butler concludes that, "The likely consequences of nuclear war have no politically, militarily or morally acceptable justification, and therefore the threat to use nuclear weapons is indefensible."

EFFECTING U.S. NUCLEAR POLICY

Even if the official history and rationalizations surrounding the 1945 atomic bombings are not rejected by a majority, these four conclusive steps—a pledge of "no first use," a promise of non-nuclear immunity, the abandonment of secret military budgets, and the renunciation of nuclear war's "usefulness"— might be taken in view of what is indisputably known about nuclear weapons. Furthermore, crucial and compelling demands have been issued . . . by dozens of authorities who now agree that nuclear abolition is necessary and possible. For example, last February at the National Press Club, 117 world leaders—among them former President Jimmy Carter, former President of the USSR Mikhail Gorbachev, former German Chancellor Helmut Schmidt, and former Canadian Prime Minister Pierre Trudeau—called upon nuclear weapons states to "declar[e] unambiguously that their goal is ultimate abolition"; in April 1997 Dr. Hans Bethe, a Nobel Prize winner and the most senior of the living scientists who built the Hiroshima and Nagasaki bombs, wrote to President Clinton calling on him to withdraw the $2.2 billion in funding set for nuclear weapons development; in December 1996, 62 retired generals and admirals from around the world published a declaration in major papers urging that "the following . . . must be undertaken now. . . . Long term international nuclear policy must be based on the declared principle of continuous, complete and irrevocable elimination of nuclear weapons."

A practical mechanism and working blueprint for verifiable nuclear disarmament was proposed August 14, 1996 by the international Canberra Commission on the Elimination of Nuclear Weapons. The commission was made up of 17 prominent experts from around the world including Gen. Butler, former Defense Secretary Robert McNamara, and Nobel Peace Prize winner Joseph Rotblat. International legal authority for such a program was reaffirmed by the July 8, 1996 Advisory Opinion of the International Court of Justice (the World Court), which (besides outlawing the threatened use of nuclear weapons) declared that nuclear weapons states are under a binding obligation to proceed with the elimination of nuclear weapons under the terms of the 1970/1995 Nuclear Non-proliferation Treaty.

These are the obvious, decisive, and available reasons and means by which to achieve the abolition of nuclear weapons. The goal can be reached only if those of us demanding it will amplify our voices and refuse to take no for an answer.

A Program to Abolish All Nuclear Weapons

THE HENRY L. STIMSON CENTER STEERING COMMITTEE
ON ELIMINATING WEAPONS OF MASS DESTRUCTION

The Henry L. Stimson Center is a nonprofit public policy institute that promotes innovative solutions to the security challenges faced by the United States and other nations. The center is named for Henry L. Stimson, who served two terms as secretary of war, one during the atomic bombing of Japan. The center's founders believe that Stimson's career in foreign and defense policy reflected his practical, nonpartisan approach toward long-range public policy goals. One of the center's major projects, Eliminating Weapons of Mass Destruction, encourages policy makers worldwide to rethink nuclear agendas.

The project's steering committee, chaired by General Andrew J. Goodpaster, consists of former and current high-ranking U.S. military and foreign policy officials and respected analysts of security policy. The following selection addresses the committee's rationale behind nuclear weapons abolition—that international accord and national security would increase—and its strategy for achieving abolition. According to the committee, by ensuring that the risks of nuclear threats outweigh the benefits, the United States and other nations can achieve a nuclear-free world.

The Cold War's end and the dangers of nuclear proliferation demand a fundamental reappraisal of the role of nuclear weapons in U.S. policy and in global politics.

In the changing strategic environment, nuclear weapons are of declining value in securing U.S. interests, but pose growing

Excerpted from "A Four-Step Program to Nuclear Disarmament," by The Henry L. Stimson Center Steering Committee on Eliminating Weapons of Mass Destruction, *Bulletin of the Atomic Scientists*, March/April 1996. Copyright © 1996 by *Bulletin of Atomic Scientists*. Reprinted with permission.

risks to the security of the United States and other nations. Their only role in this new era [1996]—the deterrence of other nuclear threats—could be met with far fewer nuclear weapons. U.S. national security would be best served by a policy of phased reductions in all states' nuclear forces and the gradual movement toward the objective of eliminating all weapons of mass destruction from all countries.

Although nuclear weapons have played a central role in foreign and defense policies for over four decades, there is no military justification in the new strategic environment for current or planned nuclear force levels. U.S. conventional forces can and should counter all conventional threats, and a combination of defensive measures and strong conventional forces are more appropriate responses to any threats of chemical and biological attacks.

The only necessary function for nuclear weapons is to deter nuclear threats to the population and territory of the United States, to U.S. forces abroad, and to certain friendly states. This deterrent function could be met at much lower force levels, as long as other states move in tandem toward smaller nuclear forces.

THE SECURITY BENEFITS OF DISARMAMENT

Deeper cuts would bring important security benefits to the United States. Aside from their direct dollar cost, the continuing existence of nuclear forces entails risks of nuclear accidents and incidents, and of the inadvertent or deliberate use of nuclear weapons in a crisis. Most importantly, continued reliance on nuclear weapons undermines international efforts to persuade other countries not to acquire nuclear weapons—the only weapons that can utterly destroy the United States as a nation and a society. Only a policy that aims at curbing global reliance on nuclear weapons—including our own—is likely to progressively eliminate nuclear dangers.

An "evolutionary" nuclear posture of careful, phased reductions, combined with an up-front, serious commitment to the long-term objective of eliminating all weapons of mass destruction, could enhance U.S. national security significantly.

The United States has committed itself to the elimination of nuclear weapons under Article VI of the Nuclear Non-Proliferation Treaty (NPT), but active governmental efforts to identify and solve the problems associated with achieving this objective have been notably lacking. A decisive commitment at the highest political level would signal to non-nuclear states that the United States' NPT pledge is real, and it would bolster important gains in recent years to devalue all weapons of mass destruction.

DISARMAMENT CAN LEAD TO THE ABOLITION OF NUCLEAR WEAPONS

The goal of elimination would be achieved in four phases, with each phase corresponding to a new strategic environment and involving changes in nuclear roles, in the operational status and size of nuclear forces, and in arms control arrangements. Alterations in the U.S. nuclear posture would be gradual and conditioned on the cooperation of other states in reducing their arsenals and strengthening nonproliferation regimes for nuclear, chemical, and biological weapons. Progress toward elimination does not imply the creation of a world government.

Phase I. In the current phase, the United States and Russia would work to reduce the importance of mutual assured destruction as a stabilizing element in their relations and would undertake cuts in their respective nuclear arsenals to roughly 2,000 warheads each. Although the United States must take into account the possibility of a reversal of reforms in Russia, the essential military role of nuclear weapons during this phase—the deterrence of nuclear attack—could be preserved at much lower force levels, and it would be beneficial for both states to undertake deeper cuts in their strategic nuclear arsenals.

Without a commitment to deeper cuts, the reductions mandated under START [Strategic Arms Reduction Talks] II will be difficult to implement in Russia. Even if reforms in Russia fail, the United States would be better off if Russia were armed with 2,000 rather than 3,500 or 6,000 deployed warheads. As U.S. and Russian arsenals are downsized, the alert status of each country's nuclear force should be reduced and new measures to increase the transparency of each nation's nuclear forces introduced. Safety issues should be given added emphasis during this phase and steps should be taken to strengthen the nonproliferation regimes for nuclear, chemical, and biological weapons. During this phase, the United States should initiate official studies of the implications of additional cuts for verification regimes and safeguards, U.S. relations with allies, conventional military forces, and the desirability and design of defensive systems.

Phase II. Stable and cordial relations among the declared nuclear weapon states would further ease the requirements for nuclear deterrence, allowing all five states to reduce their arsenals to hundreds of warheads each. As in Phase I, the only military role of nuclear weapons would be to deter nuclear attack. Nuclear weapon states, moreover, would no longer perceive nuclear weapons as contributing positively to their international status.

Cuts in force levels would be accompanied by steps to remove many, if not all, nuclear weapons from active alert status, and by the extension of nuclear transparency and safety measures to the smaller nuclear powers. Elimination of the political roles of nuclear weapons would require significant changes in U.S. defense policy, military strategy, and force posture. The United States and the other nuclear states might facilitate this transformation by deploying national defensive systems during this phase.

Phase III. All nuclear weapon states would reduce their arsenals to tens of weapons each. Achievement of the goals of this phase would require the widespread embrace of new principles and mechanisms for national security and the further marginalization of nuclear weapons in interstate relations.

Although the principle of sovereignty would be preserved, states would rely on regional and global collective security systems for their security. In such a system, nuclear weapons over time might become so devalued, yet entail so many costs, that states might prefer to act as international "trustees" of nuclear weapons. The sole function of nuclear weapons would be to deter threats of mass violence against all states and societies. When the perceived costs of maintaining such a "trustee" arrangement came to outweigh the perceived benefits, the international community would be ready to move into the final phase.

Phase IV. All nuclear weapons would be eliminated from all countries.

AN INTERNATIONAL ACCORD WOULD SUPPORT ABOLITION

Most observers find it difficult, if not impossible, to envision a nuclear-weapon-free world. Skeptics argue that the complete elimination of nuclear weapons would require an end to the principle of sovereignty in the global system and the creation of world government. In this view, as long as we live in a world of sovereign states, we are doomed to coexist with the threat of mass destruction.

We disagree. It is not too early to think hard about the issues involved. In our view, the continuation of an international system founded on state sovereignty does not imply a perpetual state of nuclear deterrence. Other outcomes would preserve the state system in recognizable form, yet offer effective alternatives to the threat of mass violence. The slow, if irregular, spread of democracy to formerly authoritarian systems could create a system in which sovereign states would remain the principal actors, but could see so little value in the threat of mass destruction that nuclear weapons and nuclear deterrence would wither away.

In order to achieve the complete elimination of all weapons of mass destruction from all countries, many serious obstacles and problems would have to be addressed and overcome. National and international verification regimes would have to be capable of detecting violations of a ban on nuclear weapons in sufficient time for the United States and the international community to mount an effective response. All relevant materials and technology would have to be subject to stringent controls, and the production of weapons–grade nuclear material and other precursor items prohibited and closely monitored.

ADDRESSING ROGUE STATES

Safeguards against the risks of a non–nuclear world would be essential. Critics of the disarmament option have argued that a non–nuclear world would be fraught with instability, since at any time some state or group might aspire to become the sole nuclear power in a world otherwise at peace. Under a worst-case scenario, a clandestine nuclear program would go unde-tected until a "rogue" state or terrorist group announced that it possessed one or more nuclear devices.

But how great are the risks of such a breakout from a dis-armament regime? Might they be countered with alternative military capabilities—both conventional forces and strategic defenses? And what political or military benefits could be ex-tracted from an announcement of nuclear acquisition in any event? Such questions deserve close study.

The safeguards regime would have to provide the interna-tional community with the appropriate tools to respond rapidly to any aggressor attempting to extract short–term gain from a position of nuclear monopoly. Under the political con-ditions envisioned for Phase IV, the detection of a violation against a global ban on weapons of mass destruction would trigger the imposition of severe economic, political, and mil-itary penalties on the perpetrator, and would likely lead to the reconstitution of nuclear forces in one or more states.

ENSURING THE RISKS OF NUCLEAR THREATS OUTWEIGH THE BENEFITS

Although a "rogue" state might threaten other countries with a nuclear, chemical, or biological attack in order to force con-cessions in the near term, any potential perpetrator would know from the outset that the benefits of blackmail would al-most certainly be short-lived. Sooner or later, the violator would face the prospect of severe penalties or certain and mas-sive retribution, depending on its actions; the short–term benefits of nuclear possession would come at the price of sure and certain reversal weeks or months later. If such a system of safeguards could be established, it is far from evident that a position of nuclear monopoly could be used to compel states to make economic, military, or other concessions in the future, although this question deserves further study.

The Naked Fear of Nuclear Disarmament

To ask one's country to relinquish its security in arms is to encourage risk—a more reasonable risk than constant nuclear escalation, but a risk nevertheless. I am struck by how much more terrified we Americans often are by talk of disarmament than by the march to nuclear war. We whose nuclear arms terrify millions around the globe are terrified by the thought of being without them. The thought of our nation without such power feels naked. Propaganda and a particular way of life have clothed us to death. To relinquish our hold on global destruction feels like risking everything, and it is risking everything—but in a direction opposite to the way in which we now risk everything. Nuclear arms protect privilege and exploitation. Giving them up would mean our having to give up economic power over other peoples. Peace and justice go together. On the path we now follow, our economic policies toward other countries require nuclear weapons. Giving up the weapons would mean giving up more than our means of global terror. It would mean giving up the reason for such terror— our privileged place in the world.

Raymond G. Hunthausen, speech delivered to the Pacific Northwest Synod of the Lutheran Church, June 12, 1981.

In the event of nuclear disarmament, it is presumed that the United States and other currently nuclear-armed states would preserve components of their nuclear arsenals under international safeguards. The only way for a violator of the ban on nuclear weapons to minimize the chances of a retaliatory strike would be to launch a preemptive attack against repositories of controlled nuclear materials and components.

If storage sites were sufficiently numerous and dispersed, such an attack would require tens of nuclear warheads. The risks that a state or group might amass enough nuclear weapons to carry out such an attack without detection by the international community could be minimized, moreover, through the acceptance of highly transparent and stringent verification regimes. The anticipated costs of cheating, in short, might so far outweigh the potential benefits of nuclear monopoly as to reduce the risk of cheating to insignificant levels, particularly if a global ban on all weapons of mass destruction were coupled with comprehensive national and international verification systems and effective regimes to safeguard against cheaters and sudden abrogators.

THE UNITED STATES MUST FULFILL ITS NPT PLEDGE

As the leading military and political power in the world, the United States bears a special responsibility to spearhead the movement to gradually decrease and, if possible, eliminate the dangers associated with nuclear weapons. Adoption of an evolutionary nuclear posture, and a revitalized commitment to the long-term objective of eliminating all nuclear weapons, could bring important national security benefits to the United States while entailing minimal risks.

Many will object to a commitment that could only be achieved, if ever, after decades. Believing the abolition of nuclear weapons to be infeasible, some would dismiss such a declaration as incredible, and therefore worthless. In this view, while it may be possible to control adequately the materials necessary to build a nuclear device, the requisite knowledge can never be eradicated. Others will argue that such a commitment might seriously compromise U.S. security interests both now and in the future. Friendly nations that now depend on our nuclear assurances might be prompted to reevaluate their nuclear forbearance, and enemies, perceiving the U.S. declaration as a sign of weakness, might be emboldened to seek nuclear weapons or to challenge U.S. interests around the world with conventional forces.

Moreover, critics might maintain that, as motives to acquire nuclear weapons cannot be eliminated, a disarmed world would be highly unstable. As long as there is no global government to guarantee the continued survival of states and to protect their interests, this view argues, the United States would be ill-advised to do away with the most powerful weapons on earth. A declaratory commitment to an objective that will only be feasible in the long term, if at all, can only divert attention and resources from steps that could be taken in the near term. In this view, a pragmatic focus on immediate steps will continue to serve U.S. interests well, and should not be hindered by attention to more radical alternatives, even as long-term possibilities.

While these objections deserve thoughtful consideration, in fact, the United States has already committed itself to the long-term objective of eliminating nuclear weapons. As a signatory to the NPT, the United States, under Article VI, is pledged to pursue "negotiations in good faith on effective measures relating to cessation of the nuclear arms race at an early date and to nuclear disarmament." That commitment was reaffirmed and made more explicit during the 1995 NPT Review Conference; tangible steps now should be taken.

Serious attention in official circles to the problems associated with going to very low levels of arsenals or to zero itself has been lacking due to the disapprobation associated with the disarmament option. Only a sustained commitment at the highest political level will legitimate serious discussions of the elimination option and ensure that resources and personnel are devoted to finding solutions to the problems associated with moving to zero, and to crafting appropriate transition strategies. In the absence of such a commitment, the nations of the world may never reach the point at which the desirability and feasibility of a nuclear-free world can be evaluated with greater certainty. To paraphrase Herman Kahn, by contemplating the unthinkable, the boundaries of the feasible might well be stretched.

In contrast, a policy concentrating only on near-term pragmatic options could raise grave dangers to U.S. security. While the existing nuclear nonproliferation regime has been remarkably robust, the status quo is unlikely to be sustainable in the long term.

Despite apocalyptic predictions of widespread proliferation, the spread of nuclear weapons, thankfully, has been contained to a handful of states. But determined countries have proven that it is possible within the current regime to acquire the necessary material and know-how to construct numbers of nuclear devices. Although the NPT was extended indefinitely in 1995, the support of many non-nuclear states was conditioned on tangible, measurable progress toward the Article VI objective of eliminating all nuclear weapons and thus on the abolition of the dual standard that sanctions nuclear possession for five states and condemns the acquisition of nuclear forces by all other participants in the regime.

Without a more radical approach to nonproliferation, the challenges posed to the nonproliferation regime can only mount over time, and the United States, eventually, is sure to face new nuclear threats.

The prospects for a nuclear-free world may be decades over the horizon. But it certainly could be achieved in one or two generations. The history of world politics since 1945 shows clearly that radical changes are possible in such a time frame. Regardless of the amount of time required, it is virtually certain that the world will never be rid of nuclear risks without a serious political commitment to the objective of progressively eliminating weapons of mass destruction from all countries. The time to start is now.

CHAPTER 3

THE MOVEMENT TO END NUCLEAR POWER

AMERICAN
SOCIAL
MOVEMENTS

The American Antinuclear Movement Evolves: 1970–1990

JEROME PRICE

During the 1970s dissent was no longer aimed solely at America's growing nuclear arsenal but began to target nuclear power as well. As reactors were being planned and built, criticism of nuclear power plants from within both the political and scientific communities raised public awareness and apprehension about the dangers of nuclear power. This increased the visibility as well as the credibility of the evolving antinuclear movement.

In the following selection Jerome Price, who holds a Ph.D. in sociology from Rutgers University, follows the rise of the movement during the early part of the decade through the early 1980s, when it gained new momentum during the pro–nuclear power presidency of Ronald Reagan.

At its peak, the movement—from coast to coast—persuaded many people to join the cause. Reasons were not hard to find. In less than a decade, the world witnessed both the calamity at Three Mile Island in Pennsylvania and the devastation at Chernobyl in the Ukraine. Price concludes that, although the movement has waned at times, it is poised for a vigorous resurgence following the developments of the 1970s and 1980s.

Almost as suddenly as the national political elite split over government reorganization to manage the energy crisis, resolution came swift and certain: the nuclear option was validated, and commitment to it was strengthened. The antinuclear movement was born, and momentum intensified from that point on.

The safety of nuclear power plants now became an important issue. The public was awakened to the controversy through a CBS broadcast about dangers in the commercial nuclear-power industry. Writing about Theodore Taylor, the physicist who had done nuclear-weapons research, John McPhee sounded the alarm in *The Curve of Binding Energy* 1974, which became essential reading for antinuclear groups forming throughout the nation.

Weakness had also been shown within the nuclear establishment. Shortly before its demise, the AEC [Atomic Energy Commission] had released the Rosenbaum report regarding the inadequacy of nuclear safeguards, then had dramatically overreacted to its own report by ordering armed guards around nuclear installations. The Monsanto Mound Laboratory in Miamisburg, Ohio, discovered that plutonium was leaking into the Erie Canal. A flood of internal memoranda were covertly released from within the AEC, confirming popular suspicion that nuclear power was not as safe or clean as proponents believed.

The government countered in 1974 by releasing a massive report on reactor safety by a research team under Norman Rasmussen at MIT [Massachusetts Institute of Technology]. Intended to be a definitive study demonstrating the statistical improbability of a nuclear accident, the Rasmussen report was immediately challenged by both the Sierra Club and the Union of Concerned Scientists—groups whose criticisms of the safety of emergency core-cooling systems in reactors had helped prepare the ground for a movement. . . .

REACHING CRITICAL MASS

Ralph Nader organized the first antinuclear conference, Critical Mass '74, in Washington, D.C. Workshops were held, and groups throughout the United States learned some of the basics of forming antinuclear organizations. At about the same time, Karen Silkwood, a worker at the Kerr–McGee plutonium-reprocessing facility in Oklahoma, was killed in an automobile accident. Her death brought the National Organization for Women and the labor movement into the antinuclear movement and cast doubt on the safety of workers in nuclear facilities. With speculation that the "accident" may have been intended, Silkwood's death also gave the movement a symbolic martyr, the first activist to die as a result of participation in the movement. This was analogous to the Kent State incident during the movement to end the Vietnam war.

Natural events also created a sense of urgency. A geologic fault that could result in an earthquake was discovered at Diablo Canyon in California, the site of a nuclear power plant under construction. In March 1975, a fire broke out at the Browns Ferry reactor in Alabama, burning through the cables controlling the emergency cooling system. If the reactor had not been shut down in time, a major nuclear accident could have occurred.

The antinuclear movement gained more attention in mid-1975, when the American Physical Society released a study critical of reactor safety. Representative Lee Aspin requested the NRC [Nuclear Regulatory Commission] to withdraw a license for the shipment of nuclear materials to South Korea, and Senator Henry Jackson publicly opposed nuclear exports to South Africa. This criticism of nuclear power from within the political and scientific establishment gave the movement credibility.

The Browns Ferry incident prompted Hugh Carey, then governor of New York, to announce his support of a nuclear moratorium in that state, and a moratorium bill was also introduced into the state legislature of Nebraska. Businessmen and Professional People in the Public Interest and the Izaak Walton League scored one of the first movement victories when they obtained a permanent stay against the Bailly, Indiana, plant construction because the site was too near major population centers. However, the stay was reversed by the U.S. Supreme Court four months later.

Local Groups Pick Up Steam

The need for international cooperation on the nuclear safeguards issue was demonstrated when West Germany announced the sale of a complete nuclear fuel cycle to Brazil, which had not signed the Nuclear Non-proliferation Treaty. President Ford responded only by asking Congress for private industry control of future uranium-enrichment plants. Local groups, however, were becoming more active on issues related to the safety of plants in the United States. In Pennsylvania, LeHigh Common Cause voted to oppose nuclear power, while the Vermont state legislature was persuaded by the Vermont Public Interest Research Group to pass a bill requiring legislative approval of new nuclear power plants. Colorado Public Interest Research Groups filed suit to force the Environmental Protection Agency (EPA) to regulate radioactive-water discharges from nuclear facilities. (Later, the U.S. Court of Appeals made the Environmental Protection Agency set water-pollution standards for all nuclear facilities.) In New York, the Safe Energy Coalition attempted to introduce a bill to prohibit the construction of any new nuclear power plants in the state but did not get legislative support, and an Iowa citizens' group blocked the licensing of a nuclear power plant until a commercial system could handle its wastes.

There was a lull in the movement during the summer of 1975 after this flurry of activity. Nuclear advocates were given a boost when Saudi Arabia announced a $15 billion electrification and desalinization plan that would include twenty-five agro-industrial complexes and a national power grid generated by nuclear power—despite the fact that uranium prices had tripled, casting doubt on the future of nuclear-fuel supply. Gulf Oil later pleaded nolo contendere to charges of price-fixing in the uranium market with the Canadian government. In other areas of controversy, the NRC officially opposed the idea of a federal security force to protect nuclear materials, challenging the argument that nuclear power would require a national security state. In New York, the Council on Economic Priorities charged Con Edison with a misleading public-relations campaign about savings from the operation of the Indian Point nuclear reactors, while Ralph Nader publicly requested the NRC and the EPA to alert two hundred New Mexico uranium miners and their families that their drinking water contained high levels of radioactive substances. Billy Jack Productions announced its intention to film a documentary on the strange circumstances surrounding Silkwood's death.

THE AMERICAN ANTINUCLEAR MOVEMENT INTENSIFIES

Everywhere the nuclear establishment was on the defensive. A group called Citizen Alert opposed an ERDA [Energy Research and Development Administration] decision choosing Nevada as the site for storage of high-level radioactive wastes. Safe Power for Maine began a petition drive for a referendum calling for a seven-year moratorium on nuclear power, while Concerned Citizens of Tennessee opposed a proposed nuclear complex in Hartsville. National Public Radio Corporation filed a Freedom of Information suit against the Justice Department to gain access to the files of its investigation into the death of Karen Silkwood, and on 13 November 1975, nuclear opponents scheduled a rally in New York City to coincide with the first anniversary of the death of Silkwood. Ralph Nader groups requested that evacuation plans in the event of a nuclear accident be released, and he coordinated efforts to block the automatic passing of uranium price increases to consumers. Two important suits were filed against the NRC with long-range implications. The Natural Resources Defense Council, the Sierra Club, and Businessmen and Professional People in the Public Interest succeeded in getting the NRC to prepare an environmental impact statement on the handling of wastes from light-water nuclear reactors. The Sierra Club and the Natural Resources Defense Council filed a petition to intervene in hearings on the Clinch River breeder reactor project, along with the East Tennessee Energy Group. The movement seemed to be gathering more support and was becoming effective in the legal arena.

November 1975 brought the second Critical Mass antinu-clear conference, with a candlelight vigil before the White House for Karen Silkwood. Ominous notes were sounded when South Africa announced its plans to construct a uranium-enrichment facility using the West German Becker jet nozzle process. And the NRC decided to allow the limited recycling of plutonium. But the following month, the National Council of Churches released a statement condemning the "plutonium economy," while the Federation of American Scientists released a poll of 10 percent of its members showing that a majority were opposed to the rapid development of nuclear power. The base of support for the antinuclear movement was broadening and becoming more inclusive of diverse segments of society.

The antinuclear movement intensified and sharpened its struggle in 1976 with a frontal attack on the nuclear establish-ment. Since 1976 was both the year of the American bicen-tennial and a presidential election, the movement's activities became even more significant.

FIGHTING EVERY LEVEL OF GOVERNMENT

The government seemed to be on the brink of finding some solutions to the nuclear-safeguards problem. An international accord was reached on nuclear exports—but then details were not announced. Nationally, the Natural Resources Defense Council appealed the NRC decision to allow the interim re-cycling of plutonium as a violation of the National Environ-mental Policy Act *and*, in a new precedent, as a violation of the Atomic Energy Act of 1954. After meeting with repre-sentatives from the National Organization for Women, Sena-tor Lee Metcalf reopened the Karen Silkwood investigation. Stop Nuclear Power of Margate, New Jersey, intervened in hearings over proposed floating nuclear power plants off the Atlantic coast. An Iowa citizens' group petitioned the NRC to revoke operating licenses for plants that repeatedly violated existing regulations. Public Media Center of California filed a suit for fairness in radio time for antinuclear advertisements.

The first major political test for the movement was the Nuclear Safeguards Initiative on the California ballot, which would take the issue directly to the people of that populous state. Early in 1976, three engineers resigned their positions in the nuclear industry to participate in the antinuclear movement in California, and a few days later a fourth engineer resigned his position in New York to work for the Union of Concerned Scientists. The resignations gave the movement a tremendous impetus, for they captured the attention of the mass media.

While the media focused on the initiative and the upcoming presidential election, antinuclear groups continued to hammer away at every level of government. The Union of Concerned Scientists, the Sierra Club, and the Natural Resources Defense Council filed a suit asking the NRC to withdraw a nuclear-export license of Edlow International Company that allowed it to ship nuclear materials to the Tarapur nuclear power plant in India. (This was eventually agreed to by President Carter, who in turn was overruled by Congress in 1980, allowing shipment to resume.) This was the first time international controls were legally sanctioned by the NRC rather than by international accord among governments. In Washington, D.C., the Silkwood case was summarily closed again, and the Supporters of Silkwood organized to focus national attention on the case. Locally, legal petitions were directed to the problem of planning for a nuclear accident. Maine Public Interest Research Group filed a show-cause order for evacuation plans in the event of an accident at Maine Yankee, and a Pennsylvania antinuclear group demanded *immediate* emergency nuclear safeguards. Friends of the Earth attempted to have the Department of Transportation in New York City stop nuclear wastes from being transported through the city until an environmental impact statement was prepared.

THE COUNTERMOVEMENT RESPONDS

As the stage was set for the confrontation in California, the National Council of Churches voted in favor of a nuclear moratorium, and the NRC released a study of terrorist and sabotage threats against nuclear installations, with the suggestion that an army unit be trained to act against terrorist groups in the event of an attack against a nuclear installation. At the site of the Indian Point reactors in New York, antinuclear activists were confronted by plant workers, who felt their jobs were being threatened by the demonstrators, prompting the formation of a group called Environmentalists for Full Employment. . . .

Utility companies throughout the nation massively infused funds into the pronuclear Citizens for Jobs and Energy organization. After a "red alert" scare to nuclear power plants on the eve of balloting day, the California Nuclear Safeguards Initiative was defeated by a two-to-one margin. The movement was not stopped; in the same month, Jimmy Carter was nominated as the Democratic presidential candidate, with a party platform supporting the development of alternatives to nuclear power. Frustrated by the failure of the tactics of legal intervention and voter referendums, however, antinuclear groups turned to direct action. The construction site of the Seabrook nuclear power plant in New Hampshire was occupied by members of the Clamshell Alliance, followed by a second demonstration with two hundred arrests. Presidential candidate Carter announced his support for civil disobedience on the part of the Seabrook activists *if* they were willing to take the consequences of their actions. These demonstrations were immediately successful: in a surprising victory for the movement, the NRC issued a temporary moratorium on new licenses until a study could be completed of nuclear-fuel reprocessing facilities and the handling of radioactive wastes. The suit had been filed by Consolidated National Intervenors, the Natural Resources Defense Council, and the New England Coalition on Nuclear Pollution.

Direct action means confrontation with authorities. Activists charged that the Federal Bureau of Investigation and the Central Intelligence Agency had monitored the activities of civilian antinuclear groups, and that the nuclear industry had funded background investigations into the Sierra Club, Friends of the Earth, Another Mother for Peace, the Union of Concerned Scientists, and Ralph Nader. . . .

ANTINUCLEAR DEMONSTRATIONS INCREASE

National attention then focused on the presidential election. Antinuclear groups prepared for referendums on the ballots in six states. Internationally, Swedish Center party leader Thorbjorn Falldin defeated the Social Democratic party in a struggle in which his opposition to nuclear power was crucial to his victory. The parents of Karen Silkwood filed a suit against the Kerr-McGee Corporation, charging company responsibility in the death of their daughter. Shortly before the elections, the NRC dramatically issued shoot-to-kill orders in the event of any attempt to sabotage fourteen nuclear-weapons facilities. The referendums' results were less than dramatic; all were soundly defeated, and the antinuclear movement was at least temporarily routed.

During 1977, the antinuclear movement persisted by relying on the tactic of demonstrations. These localized conflicts involved the nuclear power plant under construction at Seabrook, New Hampshire, and the arrest of ninety protesters at Diablo Canyon in California. The first inklings of a countermovement involving public participation came about a month after the Seabrook demonstrations, when more than three thousand construction workers and company employees who called themselves the New Hampshire Voice of Energy staged a counterdemonstration in support of nuclear power outside Seabrook, and in Charlestown, Rhode Island, pronuclear supporters disrupted a talk by Ralph Nader. . . .

Demonstrations continued at Seabrook in 1978, including one in which twenty thousand people participated. Daniel Ellsberg, veteran of the 1960s antiwar movement and the Pentagon Papers [a history of America's involvement in Vietnam written secretly in 1969 by then secretary of defense Robert S. McNamara] controversy, was one of nineteen persons arrested during a demonstration outside the military nuclear-waste dump at Rocky Flats, Colorado. The Potomac Alliance demonstrated outside the White House over the Karen Silkwood case, arrests were made outside the Trojan nuclear power plant in Oregon, and three hundred out of two thousand demonstrators of the Abalone Alliance were arrested at Diablo Canyon. The Ku Klux Klan organized a pronuclear demonstration outside Seabrook, while in the conservative South the first major demonstration took place outside the nuclear-fuel reprocessing plant in Barnwell, South Carolina, with over one thousand participants, who called themselves the Palmetto Alliance. But generally the movement was slowing down. The greatest successes were again in November: during the 1978 off-year elections, the voters of Hawaii and Montana passed limited antinuclear referenda.

FEARS ARE REALIZED

On 28 March 1979, the world was abruptly awakened to the perils of nuclear power when a complex series of human and mechanical errors resulted in the release of radioactive gases into central Pennsylvania. When the cooling system of the nuclear reactor at Three Mile Island in Harrisburg malfunctioned, the reactor core began to overheat, raising the specter of a nuclear meltdown. Reverberations from this near-disaster were immediate. Shouting "We all live in Pennsylvania," 35,000 people attended an antinuclear rally in Hanover, West Germany, to oppose plans for an underground dump for nuclear wastes. In San Francisco, demonstrators "played dead" outside a utility office, and a "die-in" was held outside the office of the Philadelphia Electric Company. Proposed bans on new nuclear power plants were introduced into state legislatures (although in Austin, Texas, voters approved a bond issue allowing the city to continue participation in a nuclear project).

The largest antinuclear rally so far took place in Washington, D.C., involving an estimated 65,000 people, following a demonstration of 20,000 people in San Francisco. According to the *New York Times* (7 May 1979) the demonstrators in Washington included representatives of the Communist party, the Socialist Worker's party, the Women's International League for Peace and Freedom, the Union of Concerned Scientists, the Grey Panthers, and the Gay Liberation Movement, among others. One month later there were more mass demonstrations throughout the world, as 5 June 1979 became designated as International Anti-Nuclear Day by movement groups. Demonstrators were arrested in Oklahoma, Arkansas, and Massachusetts. Twenty thousand Dutch citizens turned out for a rally. Six hundred protesters out of an estimated fifteen thousand were arrested outside the Shoreham, Long Island, nuclear power plant, and in Spain, one demonstrator was killed.

The size of the demonstrations and the number of people arrested grew larger and larger. In October, at Battery Park, New York, over 300,000 people turned out for a demonstration in which many movement people of the 1960s, such as Jane Fonda, reappeared. A few weeks later, 1,045 persons were arrested at the New York Stock Exchange.

But then a new crisis diverted attention from the nuclear issue. The takeover of the American Embassy in Iran and the subsequent crisis over the hostage situation "preempted" the antinuclear movement from the national media, and demonstrations were small and sporadic all through the following year....

REVIVING A WANING MOVEMENT

[The] far-reaching [pronuclear] policies and appointments [of President Ronald Reagan] did not crush the antinuclear movement but prompted it to create new tactics and strategies [during the 1980s]. The movement's focus shifted to confronting the renewed alliance between the nuclear industry and the federal government over the issues of radioactive wastes and emergency-evacuation plans for residents near nuclear power plants in the event of an accident similar to Three Mile Island. The Reagan administration sought to link the nuclear fuel cycle with the production of nuclear weapons and to overcome the last obstacles to a functional nuclear energy power system by advocating reprocessing of fuels and siting of wastes in specific states. Then an accident in the Soviet Union reawakened public opposition to nuclear power.

The Chernobyl nuclear-power-plant complex in the Ukraine, with its four operating reactors and two more under construction, is reminiscent of nuclear-energy parks once envisioned for the United States. On 26 April 1986, during an experiment to test safety systems in Unit 4, a rapid decline in power prompted operators to withdraw graphite control rods to increase the power and at the same time shut down safety systems that would interfere with the experiment. A power surge occurred, and the operators could not insert the control rods in time. In seconds, the fuel overheated and caused several massive steam explosions that tore off a one-thousand-ton containment shelter and spewed radioactive elements from the reactor core into the atmosphere: iodine-131, cesium-137, plutonium, xenon, strontium, and krypton. Thirty fires ignited near the plant. Within two days, over 130,000 people were evacuated in a nineteen-mile radius of the plant, but the evacuation was not quick enough to prevent at least 24,000 people in the path of winds carrying the radioactive debris from being exposed to dangerous levels of radiation. Twenty-nine people died of thermal burns and acute radioactive poisoning, and two others died in the explosion itself. Over three hundred people were hospitalized with serious injuries, and many received bone marrow transplants from a surgical team headed by an American, Dr. Robert Gale. Estimates of future fatalities range from a few thousand to several hundred thousand over the next several decades. . . .

The combined effect of Chernobyl and the strongly pronuclear policies of the Reagan era have set the stage for a vigorous antinuclear movement in the 1990s. The main issues are evacuation plans in the case of a nuclear accident, nuclear-waste dump sites, safety violations and cover-ups (often exposed by whistleblowers), drug abuse, the breeder reactor and nuclear-fuels reprocessing, and the production of plutonium for use in nuclear weapons. This last issue brings the antinuclear movement fully into the broader disarmament movement and creates the possibility of a merger of two seemingly disparate movements into one opposed to both nuclear energy *and* nuclear weapons.

Environmental Racism: Fighting for Nuclear Waste–Free Indian Lands

GRACE THORPE

Grace Thorpe—the daughter of legendary athlete Jim Thorpe—was a retired grandmother, living a typical life. Then, in 1991, she learned that her own tribe, Oklahoma's Sac and Fox nation, along with sixteen others, applied for grants from the U.S. Department of Energy to consider their reservations as sites for nuclear-waste storage. When, in outrage, she questioned her tribe's leaders, they simply replied that their tribe "could use the money."

Within a year, this grandmother became a leading antinuclear activist for Native Americans in the United States, Canada, and Mexico. She founded the National Environmental Coalition of Native-Americans, which urges tribes to set up nuclear-free zones on their reservations, and has brought the concepts of radioactive and environmental racism into the antinuclear debate.

In the following speech, delivered at the North American Native Workshop on Environmental Justice in March 1995, Thorpe explores the history of devastation on the reservations due to nuclear energy and discusses the sociopolitical maneuvering behind the U.S. government's motivation to store nuclear waste on Indian land: "In rich areas, people have the leisure time to organize an easy access to media and elected representatives. For this reason, *the nuclear industry is talking about locating disposal sites in poor regions.*" Thorpe laments this corruption of her people's heritage: "Is this the legacy that we want to leave for our children and for our Mother Earth?"

Excerpted from Grace Thorpe's speech delivered at the North American Native Workshop on Environmental Justice, Iliff School of Theology, Denver, March 17, 1995. Copyright © 1995 by Grace Thorpe. Reprinted with permission.

The Great Spirit instructed us that, as Native people, we have a consecrated bond with our Mother Earth. We have a sacred obligation to our fellow creatures that live upon it. For this reason it is both painful and disturbing that the United States government and the nuclear power industry seem intent on forever ruining some of the little land we have remaining. The nuclear waste issue is causing American Indians to make serious, possibly even genocidal, decisions concerning the environment and the future of our peoples.

I was a corporal, stationed in New Guinea, at the end of World War II when the first atomic bomb was dropped on Hiroshima. The so-called "nuclear-age" has passed in the beat of a heart. As impossible as it seems, this year [1995] will mark the fiftieth anniversary of that first blast. The question of what to do with the waste produced from the commercial and military reactors, involved in weapons manufacture and the generation of nuclear energy, has stumped the minds of the most brilliant physicists and scientists since "Little Boy" was detonated above Japan on August 6, 1945. *No* safe method has yet been found for the disposal of such waste, the most lethal poison known in the history of humanity. It remains an orphan of the nuclear age.

In rich areas, people have the leisure time to organize an easy access to media and elected representatives. For this reason, *the nuclear industry is talking about locating disposal sites in poor regions.* Indians are being deluged by requests. Devastation due to nuclear energy, however, is nothing new to Indian peoples.

Between 1950 and 1980, approximately 15,000 persons worked in uranium mines. One-fourth of these were Indian. Many of these mines were located on lands belonging to the Navajos and the Pueblos. In 1993, Dr. Louise Abel of the Indian Health Service disclosed that, of the 600 miners tested who had worked underground for more than a year, only 5 qualified for payments under the Radiation Exposure Act of 1990. By 1994, only 155 uranium miners and millers or their families had been awarded compensation, less than half the claims filed at that time. Radiation from tailings piles, the debris left after the uranium is extracted, has leached into groundwater that feeds Indian homes, farms, and ranches. High concentrations of radon gas continually seep out of the piles and are breathed by Natives in the area. Background levels of radiation are at dangerous levels. Thus Indians living near the mines face the same health risks as those working underground.

In 1973 and 1974, two nuclear power reactors commenced operation at Prairie Island, Minnesota, only a few hundred yards from the homes, businesses, and child care center of the Prairie Island Mdewankanton Sioux. The facility was on the site of the ancient Indian village and burial mound, dating back at least 2,000 years. On October 2, 1979, a 27-minute release of radiation from the plants forced evacuation of the facility, but the tribe was not notified until several days later. By 1989, radioactive tritium was detected in the drinking water, forced the Mdewankanton to dig an 800-foot deep well and water tower, completed in 1993. Prairie Island residents are exposed to six times the cancer risk deemed acceptable by the Minnesota Department of Health.

By 1986, the problem of nuclear waste disposal had become acute. The U.S. Department of Energy (DOE) began to explore the possibility of locating a permanent nuclear repository in Minnesota's basalt and granite hardrock deposits. Among the sites considered was the White Earth Reservation in the northwestern part of the state. The Anishiaabe who live there took the government's interest seriously enough to commission a study of the potential impact. The Minnesota legislature responded by passing the Radioactive Waste Management Act, stating that no such facility could be located within the state without the express authorization of the legislature.

The following year, however, Congress voted to locate the permanent repository at Yucca Mountain, about 100 miles northwest of Las Vegas, Nevada, on land belonging to the Western Shoshone. Plans called for the opening of the facility in 2010. The Nuclear Waste Policy Act set in motion a nationwide search for a community that would accept a temporary site, until Yucca Mountain came online. *Indian tribes again were specifically targeted.*

TAKING A STAND: CREATING NUCLEAR FREE ZONES

One by one, tribes who considered accepting the so-called Monitored Retrievable Storage (MRS) facility on tribal land decided against it. Today, of the 17 tribes who began discussions and study, only three remain: the Mescalero Apache of New Mexico, the Goshutes in Utah, and the Fort McDermitt Reservation in Nevada (which houses both Paiutes and Western Shoshones). In addition, Pojoaque Pueblo in New Mexico announced in March 1995 that it was considering locating the MRS on tribal lands. This move, however, was an overt power play to persuade the New Mexico legislature to halt a bill that would expand gambling in the state to the detriment of the Pojoaque's own gambling interests. According to Pojoaque Governor Jacob Viarrial, "If the public does not want his tribe to store the waste, they should put pressure on the lawmakers to put a halt to the expansion of gaming off reservations."

The National Environmental Coalition of Native Americans (NECONA) was formed in 1993 in Las Vegas to lobby against the MRS or any nuclear waste disposal on Indian lands and to encourage Native Nations to declare themselves Nuclear Free Zones instead. As the number of tribes considering the MRS dwindled, pressure on Washington mounted. NECONA persuaded U.S. Senator Jeff Bingaman of New Mexico, who had been one of the moving forces behind the Radiation Exposure Compensation Act for uranium miners, to oppose the MRS on the energy and the appropriations committees. As a result, Congress withheld funding for the program.

With the federal government out of the MRS-construction business, but with the problem of waste disposal still unresolved, utilities began to get desperate. Dozens of plants would be forced to shut-down or find alternative sources of fuel unless a temporary storage site were located in the near future. Thirty-three utilities, accounting for 94 reactors, began seeking a location. Led by Northern States Power (NSP), the consortium approached Minnesota about locating a facility adjacent to the NSP plant at Prairie Island. Although the plant supplies 15% of the state's electricity, "not a single kilowatt reaches the Mdewankanton community it borders."

The Prairie Island Sioux had applied for a Phase I MRS grant, which provided DOE funds for initial feasibility studies. According to tribal officials, however, the application was tactical. The intent was to use the government's own money to prove that neither an MRS nor a nuclear power plant should be located at Prairie Island. One study showed that the cancer risk would be 23 times greater than the state standard. At the time of the NSP initiative, a survey showed that 91.6 percent of the tribe opposed construction of the MRS. The tribe fought the NSP proposal before the legislature and won. They subsequently declared the Prairie Island Reservation a Nuclear Free Zone.

Meanwhile, NSP has signed an agreement with the Mescalero Apache to move ahead with development of an MRS in New Mexico. Under the terms of the agreement, the tribe was to seek two 20-year licenses to store up to 40,000 metric tons of spent nuclear fuel. Total revenues over the 40-year life of the facility, estimated at $2.3 billion, would bring as much as $250 million in benefits to the tribe. The tribal council believed that it could proceed with the program by its own authority, it was confident enough of victory to put the issue to tribal members in the form of a public referendum. According, however, to a Native Newspaper, *The Circle*, opponents of the storage facility considered the Mescalero tribal government, headed by Chairman Wendall Chino, "dictatorial, and likely to conduct a campaign of intimidation and vote fraud if a referendum takes place."

The Mescalero don't need this nuclear waste. They have a five-star resort, a casino, two ski lifts, forestry resources, and a sawmill.

The referendum took place January 31, 1995. The Mescaleros voted down the MRS by a vote of 490 to 362. Shortly after the vote, however, a petition began circulating, calling for a new election. According to Fred Peso, the vice chairman, "A group of grass-roots people presented the petition to the tribal council." Peso blamed "outside interference from environmentalists and other anti-tribal groups" for the defeat of the proposal. In reality, Wendall Chino's powerful political machine was behind the petition. The tribal government controls jobs, housing, schools, and the court system. One of the organizers of the petition drive, Fred Kaydahzinne, is director of the federally subsidized tribal housing program. As Rufina Marie Laws, one of the referendum's opponents, stated, "It was real hard for people to turn him down." Petition organizers gathered more than 700 signatures calling for a new vote. When a second ballot was held on March 9, 1995, the measure passed 593 to 372.

There is a great deal of uncertainty as to what will happen now at Mescalero. Opponents of the MRS could seek yet another referendum. They have stated that they will appeal the second vote to the tribal court, but they are not optimistic. The state of New Mexico has prohibited transport of spent nuclear fuel on state highways, in an attempt to derail the proposal. Vice Chairman Peso has announced that the tribe will proceed with licensing applications and technological studies. Officials of NSP have announced that they will move ahead with plans for the project. Contracts are being finalized, and licensing is anticipated to be concluded by December 1996.

If the Mescaleros withdraw, there are the Skull Valley Goshutes in Utah and the tribes at Fort McDermitt standing right behind them. Both reservations are isolated, and unemployment is a problem on both. At the moment, Fort McDermitt seems to be out of the running because it straddles the Nevada state line. The law says that the MRS and the permanent site cannot be in the same state, but that could change. The Goshutes already have waste incinerators, nerve gas plants, and a bombing range bordering their lands. There is a feeling of indifference about the MRS among the few people who live on the reservation. They have signed an accord with Richard Stallings, a federal negotiator charged with locating a temporary storage site, to provide a framework for further talks, and the University of Utah has agreed to undertake a feasibility study with the utilities.

We should also not believe that the problem is limited to the United States. First Nations in Canada are facing the issue. An article in the free trade agreement between Canada and the United States prohibits Canada from preventing nuclear waste coming into the country. The Meadow Lake Cree in Saskatchewan are in discussion with the Atomic Energy of Canada Ltd. (AECL), a corporation of the Canadian government, concerning becoming a permanent repository. According to recent reports, they have also held negotiations with the Mescalero to become the storage site for wastes temporarily housed at the proposed Arizona facility. Meanwhile, AECL continues to market nuclear technology throughout the Americas. The situation in Mexico is terrible. They have very little environmental regulation.

Tribal officials at Mescalero and other reservations that have considered the MRS contend that the issue is one of sovereignty. They use the issue of sovereignty against the environment. It is a very tough tightrope to walk. How can you say to a tribe, "Hey, you shouldn't be doing this. You should be protecting the earth." Then they would turn around and reply, "Hey, we can do as we please. This is Indian sovereignty." In one sense, they would be right. Allowing utilities to build MRS facilities on our lands, however, is not truly an expression of sovereignty. Those supporting such sites are selling our sovereignty. The utilities are using our names and our trust lands to bypass environmental regulations. The issue is not sovereignty. The issue is Mother Earth's preservation and survival. The issue is environmental racism. The purpose of NECONA is to invite tribes to express their sovereign national rights in a more creative way in favor of our Mother, by joining the growing number of tribal governments that are choosing to declare their lands Nuclear Free Zones. Fred Peso at Mescalero has declared, "It is ironic that the state continues to fight our tribe (over the MRS) when New Mexico has enjoyed the benefits of nuclear projects since 1945." The real irony is that after years of trying to destroy it, the United States is promoting Indian national sovereignty—just so they can dump their waste on Native land.

The DOE and the utilities have said that it is natural that we, as Native peoples, should accept radioactive waste on our lands. They have convinced some of our traditionalists that as keepers of the land they must accept it. As Russell Means has said, however, "We have always had our false prophets." The government and the nuclear power industry attempt to flatter us about our abilities as "earth stewards." Yet as I declared to the National Congress of American Indians in 1993, "It is a perversion of our beliefs and an insult to our intelligence to say that we are 'natural stewards' of these wastes." The real intent of the government and the utilities is to rid themselves of this extremely hazardous garbage on Indian lands so they are free to generate more of it.

IGNORING THE PAST, ENDANGERING THE FUTURE

Our traditional spiritual leaders have warned us for hundreds of years about taking resources from the earth. They have warned that the earth will become unbalanced and be destroyed. In one of the stories the Navajos have about their origins, they were warned about the dangers of uranium. The People "emerged from the third world into the fourth and present world and were given a choice. They were told to choose between two yellow powders. One was yellow dust from the rocks, and the other was corn pollen. The [People] chose corn pollen, and the gods nodded in assent. They also issued a warning. Having chosen the corn pollen, the Navajos were to leave the yellow dust in the ground. If it was ever removed, it would bring evil."

Wherever there are uranium mines, wherever there are nuclear power plants, and wherever our people have been downwind on nuclear tests, the cancer rate goes up. Among the Western Shoshone in Nevada as a result of nuclear testing, many of the people now have thyroid cancer. They are dying a younger death. They have leukemia, which was unheard of in earlier times. Pollution and toxic waste from the Hanford nuclear weapons facility threatens all Native peoples who depend on the Columbia River salmon for their existence. A few years ago, a vial of nuclear material the size of a human finger was lost on the road from Los Angeles to Sacramento. An SOS went out to the media about this little silver vial: If you find it, don't pick it up. Alert us immediately. If you pick it up and put it in your pocket for two days, you'll get sick. If you keep it a week, it can kill you. If you breathe a 100th of a grain of salt, it can cause lung cancer."

Now those who visited all these horrors upon us want us to accept their nuclear waste, too. Darelynn Lehto, the vice president of the Prairie Island Mdewankanton, testified before the Minnesota State Senate during the fight against MRS there, "It is the worst kind of environmental racism to force our tribe to live with the dangers of nuclear waste simply because no one else is willing to do so." Why do we tolerate it? How long can we tolerate it? What kind of society permits the manufacture of products that cannot be safely disposed? NECONA is currently lobbying Congress for a bill that will say simply, "Nothing is to be manufactured, used, or reproduced in the United States that cannot be safely disposed of." Is that too simple a thing for a legislator to understand? Probably it is, but it makes sense, doesn't it?

Is This Our Legacy?

Spent nuclear fuel is permeated with plutonium, the principal ingredient in atomic weapons. Plutonium has a half life of 24,360 years. Significant amounts would therefore remain active for more than 50,000 years. The so-called permanent repository proposed for Yucca Mountain is designed to hold canisters containing nuclear waste for only 10,000 years. The steel containers holding the material would disintegrate long before the radioactivity had decayed.

Yucca Mountain, however, is nowhere near on its way to becoming the permanent repository. It was originally to have begun receiving waste in 1998, but near unanimous opposition in Nevada slowed the process. In 1992, an earthquake measuring 5.6 on the Richter scale struck the area, raising additional questions as to the site's viability. Most recently, scientists at the Los Alamos National Laboratory in New Mexico raised the possibility that wastes buried at the Nevada location could explode after the steel container canisters dissolve, setting off a nuclear chain reaction.

These factors make the targeted date of 2010—when Yucca Mountain currently is estimated to be accepting shipments of waste—look improbable. Mescalero tribal officials, in obtaining their tribe's permission, emphasized that their proposed facility was strictly temporary and that "at no time would the tribe take possession of the fuel." What will happen, however, if Yucca Mountain does not come online as projected? What if no permanent storage site is available at the end of the MRS' 40 years of "temporary" storage? New Mexico Attorney General Tom Udall has raised similar questions. He fears that the state "may ultimately have to pick up the pieces." Indians suspect we know who will be left holding the bag.

The debate over nuclear waste has already done serious damage to harmonious relationships among our people. Why must we go through this divisive agony again?

As a mother and a grandmother, I am concerned about the survival of our people just as Mother Earth is concerned about the survival of her children. There is currently a moratorium on construction of nuclear power plants in the United States. There is also current legislation, however, that would allow new building if arrangements are made for the waste. Is this the legacy that we want to leave for our children and for our Mother Earth? The Iroquois say that in making any decision one should consider the impact for seven generations to come. As Thom Fassett, who is Iroquois, reminds us, taking such a view on these issues often makes us "feel we are alone, rolling a stone up a hill. It keeps rolling back down on us." That may be the only way, however, for us to live up to our sacred duty to the land and to all of creation.

Unsafe Reactors Jeopardize Public Safety

David Lochbaum

David Lochbaum is the nuclear safety engineer for the Union of Concerned Scientists (UCS), which has worked since 1969 to reduce the risks from nuclear power, promote alternatives to nuclear energy, and rid the world of nuclear weapons. The UCS is also a member of the Coalition to Reduce Nuclear Dangers, which advocates the reduction of existing nuclear arsenals and the prevention of new nuclear developments.

Lochbaum monitors and reports on nuclear power safety issues for the UCS. He presented the following testimony to the Clean Air, Wetlands, Private Property, and Nuclear Safety subcommittee of the U.S. Senate on May 8, 2001. In it, he criticizes the Nuclear Regulatory Commission (NRC) for being lax in enforcing updates and repairs to aging plants, the publication of plant-specific risk studies, and improving plant security forces. This failure by the NRC jeopardizes public safety, and Lochbaum cites it as just cause for the government to intervene and reform the NRC before another Three Mile Island, Chernobyl disaster, or terrorist attack endangers the United States.

T he Union of Concerned Scientists (UCS) . . . seeks to ensure that all people have clean air, energy and transportation, as well as food that is produced in a safe and sustainable manner. We have worked on nuclear plant safety issues for nearly 30 years. In fact, far too many of the safety issues that I

Excerpted from David Lochbaum's testimony to the U.S. Senate Subcommittee on Clean Air, Wetlands, Private Property, and Nuclear Safety, www.ucsusa.org, May 8, 2001.

work on today were also worked on by my predecessor, Robert Pollard, and his predecessors, Daniel Ford and Henry Kendall. This experience convinces us that the United States should not consider an expanded role for nuclear power until we achieve something that we have never had—namely, a consistently effective regulator.

The Nuclear Regulatory Commission (NRC) has exclusive responsibility for regulating safety at US nuclear power plants. That the last US reactor meltdown happened 22 years ago (Three Mile Island) is circumstantial evidence that the NRC is not always an inept regulator. On the other hand, there is mounting circumstantial evidence in areas such as nuclear plant license renewal, steam generator tube cracking, risk-informed regulation, and nuclear plant security indicating that the NRC is not always an effective regulator either. These warning signs are described in the following sections.

PLANT LICENSE RENEWAL UNCHECKED

The NRC currently approves a 20-year extension to the original 40-year license for a nuclear plant after its owner "demonstrates that a nuclear power plant facility's structures and components requiring aging management review in accordance with §54.21(a) for license renewal have been identified and that the effects of aging on the functionality of such structures and components will be managed to maintain the CLB [current licensing bases] such that there is an acceptable level of safety during the period of extended operation." In theory, this demonstration seems like a solid basis for continued safe operation. In reality, this demonstration amounts to little more than a paperwork exercise that is frequently contradicted by actual experience. Since the beginning of the 21st century, at least eight nuclear power plants have been forced to shut down due to equipment failures caused by aging:

- March 7, 2000: The owner reported that Nine Mile Point Unit 2 in New York had automatically shut down when the system controlling the level of water over the reactor core failed. The owner attributed the failure as "Specifically, the manual-tracking card failed to provide an output signal when the feedwater master controller was switched from automatic to manual mode of operation. . . . The manual-tracking card failed due to *aging.*" [emphasis added]

- March 14, 2000: The owner reported that Catawba Unit 1 in South Carolina had automatically shut down due to an inadvertent electrical ground problem. The owner reported "A detailed failure analysis determined that the root cause of the connector failure was the misapplication of the connector insert insulating material which is made of neoprene. . . . The neoprene insert at the failure point on the connector exhibits signs of *accelerated aging* [emphasis added]. The inserts are hardened and there are charred deposits on the end of the inserts which are indications of electrical tracking."

- March 17, 2000: The owner reported that Indian Point Unit 2 in New York had been forced to declare an emergency condition and shut down after a steam generator tube failed and resulted in approximately 19,197 gallons leaking from the reactor coolant system. The owner stated "Preliminary analysis indicates that the cause of the tube failure is primary water stress corrosion cracking (PWSCC)" [i.e., aging].

- March 27, 2000: The owner reported that Catawba Unit 2 in South Carolina had automatically shut down due to an inadvertent electrical ground problem. The owner reported "A detailed failure analysis determined that the root cause of the connector failure was the misapplication of the connector insert insulating material which is made of neoprene. . . . The neoprene insert at the failure point on the connector exhibits signs of *accelerated aging* [emphasis added]. The inserts are hardened and there are charred deposits on the end of the inserts which are indications of electrical tracking."

- September 12, 2000: The owner reported that Oyster Creek in New Jersey had been forced to shut down be-

WHERE NUCLEAR POWER PLANTS AGE

Aging and worn equipment at the nation's 120 nuclear power plants has led to a series of fires, radiation and steam leaks, and other accidents. Here is how old nuclear plants are failing:

Weakened tension wires
● Containment structure prevents release of radioactive gases in a nuclear accident.
● Tension wires that support integrity of structure have weakened or broken.
● Seven plants have compromised wires.

Reactor cracks
● Control rod nozzles limit the speed and heat of a nuclear reaction.
● Reactor cracks around nozzles could lead to ejection of control rods and loss of coolant that would threaten nuclear core.
● At least five reactors have experienced cracks.

Cracked steam generator
● In pressurized-water reactors, tubes separate clean water from radioactive contaminants.
● Cracks or failures in tubes could allow radioactive material to leak into cooling water.
● Six steam generators have ruptured, including one in Indian Point, NY, which failed last year and leaked radioactive gas into atmosphere.

Aging, corroded pipes
● Leaks from cooling pipes and safety valves, due to corrosion or aging, could allow radioactive water to leak outside containment structure.
● At least 20 plants have experienced such leaking. In two cases, radioactive water leaked outside containment structure.

Electrical failures
● Nuclear plant safety systems are powered and controlled by electrical devices.
● Devices are aging and can fail, compromising control of safety systems.
● At least 14 plants have experienced failures. At Diablo Canyon last year, and San Onofre in February, electrical failures sparked fires that shut down safety systems.

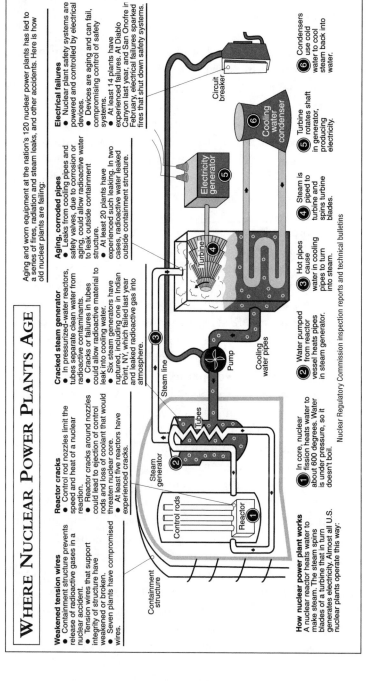

How nuclear power plant works
A nuclear reactor heats water to make steam. The steam spins blades of a turbine that in turn generates electricity. Almost all U.S. nuclear plants operate this way:

① In core, nuclear fission heats water to about 600 degrees. Water is under pressure, so it doesn't boil.

② Water pumped from reactor vessel heats pipes in steam generator.

③ Hot pipes cause water in cooling pipes to turn into steam.

④ Steam is piped to turbine and spins turbine blades.

⑤ Turbine rotates shaft in generator, producing electricity.

⑥ Condensers use cold water to cool steam back into water.

Nuclear Regulatory Commission inspection reports and technical bulletins cause a system needed to provide containment integrity had failed a periodic test. The owner determined "The cause of the degradation in Secondary Containment was *age-related degradation* [emphasis added] of the automatic ventilation exhaust valve seals."

- September 27, 2000: The NRC reported that Diablo Canyon Unit 1 in California had automatically shut down after an electrical transformer failed and interrupted the supply of electricity to the reactor coolant pumps. The NRC stated "The licensee's evaluation concluded that a center bus bar overheated at a splice joint, which caused a polyvinyl chloride boot insulator over the splice joint to smoke. Eventually, heat-induced failure of fiberglass insulation on adjacent phases resulted in phase-to-phase arcing" [i.e., aging].

- February 16, 2001: The owner reported that North Anna Unit 2 in Virginia had been forced to shut down due to leakage exceeding ten gallons per minute from the reactor coolant system. The owner determined "The cause of the stem packing material failure below the lantern ring is attributed to *aging*" [emphasis added].

- April 2, 2001: The owner reported that San Onofre Unit 3 in California automatically shut down after an electrical breaker failed and started a fire. The failed breaker was reportedly 25 years old and scheduled for inspection *next* year. The owner "will implement modifications to appropriate *preventative maintenance* [emphasis added] procedures to address the apparent failure causes."

Aging management programs are intended to monitor the condition of equipment and structures and implement repairs or replacements when necessary to prevent failures. The cited aging-related failures, occurring about once every 60 days, indicate beyond reasonable doubt that the aging management programs are inadequate because they are *not* preventing equipment failures. The NRC must ascertain the effectiveness of aging management programs—not merely the scope of these programs—*before* granting license extensions.

Steam Generator Tube Cracking

Dr. Joram Hopenfeld, who recently retired from the NRC staff, raised concerns about the integrity of steam generator tubes to his management nearly ten years ago. The agency—which steadfastly *claims* that safety is its top priority—essentially ignored them until an accident last year at Indian Point 2. The ensuing public outcry and Congressional attention resulting from that accident, which was initiated when a cracked steam generator tube failed, forced the NRC to dust off Hopenfeld's concerns and finally look into them. The NRC asked its Advisory Committee on Reactor Safeguards (ACRS) to evaluate the decade-old concerns.

ACRS issued a report in February 2001. The ACRS substantiated many of Dr. Hopenfeld's concerns. For example, the ACRS concluded:

- "The techniques [used to look for cracked steam generator tubes] are not nearly so reliable for determining the depth of a crack, and in particular, whether a crack penetrates through 40% of the tube wall thickness." [NRC's regulations do not allow a nuclear plant to start up with any steam generator tube cracked more than 40 percent of its wall thickness, but the methods used to inspect the tubes for cracks cannot reliably determine the depth of cracks.]
- "The NRC staff acknowledged that there would be some possibility that cracks of objectionable depth might be overlooked and left in the steam generator for an additional operating cycle." *[Exactly what actually happened at Indian Point 2 to cause last year's accident.]*
- "Both the [NRC] staff and the author of the DPO [differing professional opinion] [Dr. Hopenfeld] agree that the alternative repair criteria [used by the NRC staff to allow nuclear plants to continue operating with steam generator tubes known to be cracked] increase the probability of larger primary-to-secondary flows during the MSLB [main steam line break] and SGTR [steam generator tube rupture] accidents."
- "The [ACRS] also finds that this contention of the DPO

[namely, that an accident at a nuclear plant with cracked steam generator tubes could cause those tubes to completely break] has merit and deserves investigation."

- "This seems to be a plausible contention [that an accident at a nuclear plant with cracked steam generator tubes could widen the cracks and result in larger leakage], and the staff has not produced analyses or test results to refute it."

- "The [ACRS] concluded that the issue of the possible evolution of severe accident to involve gross failure of steam generator tubes and bypass of the containment is not yet resolved . . . [and] that the issue needs consideration regardless of the criteria adopted for the repair and replacement of steam generator tubes."

- "Data available to the [ACRS] suggest that the constant probability of detection [of cracked steam generator tubes] adopted by the NRC staff is nonconservative for flaws producing voltage signals less than about 0.7 volts." *[In other words, the NRC staff assumes that methods used to find cracked tubes are much better than the data shows them to be.]*

- "The [ACRS] was unable to identify defensible technical bases for the [NRC] staff decisions to not consider the correlation of the iodine spiking factor with initial iodine concentration [when evaluating the potential offsite radiation dose consequences from accidents involving cracked steam generator tubes]."

- "The [ACRS] found that the [NRC] staff did not have a technically defensible understanding of these processes to assess adequately the potential for procession of damage to steam generator tubes." *[In other words, the NRC staff has no sound basis for arguing that one broken tube will not cascade and cause the failures of other tubes.]*

- "The [NRC] staff has not developed persuasive arguments to show that steam generator tubes will remain intact under conditions of risk-important accidents in which the reactor coolant system remains pressurized. The current analyses dealing with loop seals in the coolant system are not yet adequate risk assessments."

- "In developing assessments of risk concerning these design basis accidents, the [NRC] staff must consider the probabilities of multiple tube ruptures until adequate technical arguments have been developed to show damage progression is improbable." *[In other words, the risk studies to date, which only consider failure of a single tube, may understate the true risk and therefore should not be relied upon.]*

The concerns raised by Dr. Hopenfeld are extremely important safety issues. As the ACRS stated:

- "Steam generators constitute more than 50% of the surface area of the primary pressure boundary in a pressurized water reactor."
- "Unlike other parts of the reactor pressure boundary, the barrier to fission product release provided by the steam generator tubes is not reinforced by the reactor containment as an additional barrier."
- "Leakage of primary coolant through openings in the steam generator tubes could deplete the inventory of water available for the long-term cooling of the core in the event of an accident."

In the decade since Dr. Hopenfeld first raised his safety concerns, the NRC has allowed many nuclear plants to continue operating, nuclear power plants with literally thousands of steam generator tubes known to be cracked. The ACRS concluded that the NRC staff made these regulatory decisions using incomplete and inaccurate information. After receiving the ACRS's report, the NRC staff considered Hopenfeld's concerns "resolved" even though it had taken no action to address the numerous recommendations in the ACRS report.

The NRC must REALLY resolve Dr. Hopenfeld's concerns as soon as possible. In the interim, the NRC must stop making decisions affecting the lives of millions of Americans when it lacks "defensible technical bases."

RISK-INFORMED REGULATION IS A MUST

Two of the NRC's four strategic goals are to maintain safety and to reduce unnecessary regulatory burden. The agency attempts to define "unnecessary" using plant-specific risk studies that purportedly draw a nice clean line between what is necessary and what is not. But UCS released a report titled "Nuclear Plant Risk Studies: Failing the Grade" last August detailing numerous flaws in the publicly available plant-specific risk studies. Among other flaws, we compared the risk study results for three sets of nearly identical plants and found that they varied widely—not because the risks were that disparate but because different assumptions and methods were used. Consequently, it is extraordinarily easy to move that nice clean line simply by tweaking a few input assumptions and have a burden appear as either necessary or unnecessary.

For example, the FitzPatrick nuclear plant in New York had a problem three or four years ago with a valve that must open following a certain accident to provide cooling flow to the reactor core. But the valve's motor did not develop sufficient thrust to move the valve against the high pressure that would occur if that accident happened. Fixing the valve was therefore a very necessary burden. Yet the plant's owner went back to the risk study and re-calculated the risk from that accident happening concurrently with a complete failure of the electrical grid and adjusted the line until the burden became "unnecessary." This example is not sharpening one's pencil because the accident in question happens most frequently when the electrical grid remains available. Thus, this vital safety system would not have functioned properly for the most likely accident scenario.

More recently, the NRC staff allowed Fermi Unit 2 in Michigan to continue operating after the company broke one of its emergency diesel generators due to either incompetence or negligence. The company submitted a risk study to the NRC staff that showed the continued operation increased the threat of an accident. But the NRC staff discounted that quantified threat by saying that the unquantified threat from shutting down and then restarting the nuclear reactor would somehow pose an even larger threat. This NRC decision contradicts its own regulations, policies, and procedures and UCS has asked the NRC's Inspector General to investigate this matter.

The plant-specific risk studies that UCS reviewed for our report are nearly ten years old, but they are the most recent risk studies that are publicly available. The NRC is allowing plant owners to reduce the testing frequency for emergency equipment or to continue operating with degraded equipment based on results from more recent risk studies. The previously cited ACRS report on Hopenfeld's steam generator tube integrity concerns indicates that the more recent risk studies remain inaccurate and incomplete. Members of the public and organizations like UCS cannot challenge these regulatory decisions because we lack access to the risk studies. The NRC's own regulations, policies, and procedures require such information to be publicly available, but it is not. And the agency continues to make regulatory decisions affecting the lives of millions of Americans in a vacuum. The NRC must require the flaws in the risk studies to be corrected *AND* make sufficient information about the corrected risk studies publicly available.

NUCLEAR PLANT SECURITY IS LAX

The NRC's handling of physical security at nuclear reactors is another example of regulatory ineffectiveness. The NRC began force-on-force tests of security preparedness at nuclear power plants in the early 1990s. These tests pit a handful of simulated intruders against a plant's physical defenses and squadrons of armed security personnel. By 1998, these tests had revealed significant security weaknesses in about 47 percent of the plants tested. The NRC quietly discontinued the testing, but the ensuing public outrage forced the agency to re-institute the tests. Since the tests have been resumed, about 47 percent of the plants continue to have significant security flaws revealed. Last year, force-on-force tests at the Waterford plant in Louisiana and the Quad Cities plant in Illinois demonstrated serious security problems that warranted extensive repairs and upgrades. The owner of the Waterford spent more than $2 million fixing its inadequate security system.

Having been foiled in its attempt to secretly deep-six the

security tests, the agency resorted to Plan B in which they will allow the plant owners to conduct the tests themselves, grade the tests themselves, and simply mail in the scores—virtually guaranteed to be high marks—to the NRC. If someone like [Oklahoma City bomber] Timothy McVeigh drove to a nuclear power plant with intentions of causing harm, the people living near that plant would be better protected by security scoring 85 percent on a real test than 100 or even 110 percent on an open-book, take-home, self-scored test. The public deserves and must get that better protection than that provided by artificially inflated security test scores.

NEW PLANT DESIGN PROVES RISKY

A new nuclear technology called the pebble-bed modular reactor is getting considerable mention as the type of nuclear reactor most likely to be built in the United States in the future. The pebble-bed reactor does offer certain safety advantages— at least, on paper. Proponents claim that the pebble-bed reactor cannot experience the meltdown-type accident as occurred at Three Mile Island in 1979. Perhaps, but can the pebble-bed reactor, which will use more graphite in each reactor module than is presently used in all existing US nuclear power plants combined, catch on fire and burn as happened at Windscale in 1957 and Chernobyl in 1986? Can plant workers, either by mistake or by design, trigger an accident as occurred at the SL-1 nuclear reactor in 1961 and Dresden Unit 3 in 1974 and Browns Ferry in 1975? Can some unexpected component failure cause fuel damage, as occurred at Fermi Unit 1 in 1966?

The pebble-bed reactor is rumored to be competitive with other energy technologies. It appears from a preliminary design review that the proposed reactor achieves its economic advantages by replacing the steel-lined, reinforced-concrete containment structures used for our existing nuclear plants with a far less robust enclosure building. The NRC's own Advisory Committee on Reactor Safeguards characterized this as "a major safety trade-off."

The safety problem with the proposed "containment-lite"

pebble-bed reactor design is compounded by the existing security weaknesses. Imagine the consequences from a fertilizer truck bomb detonated next to a "containment-lite" reactor with millions of curies of lethal radioactivity to contaminate the environment for many decades. That would truly be a nuclear nightmare.

Cost projections by the nuclear industry must be taken with a grain of salt, if not an entire salt shaker. According to the US Department of Energy, the actual construction costs for 75 nuclear power plants started between 1966 and 1977 were more than three times higher than their estimated costs. Thus, claims that the projected costs of electricity from a proposed pebble-bed reactor are competitive with the actual costs of electricity from operating renewable energy technologies must be viewed with skepticism.

It cannot be overemphasized that a facility like the proposed pebble-bed modular reactor has never been constructed or operated in the world. Consequently, its expected performance characteristics are highly speculative. It would not be prudent at this time to place undue reliance on a risky technology with unproven safety performance. Nuclear experiments belong in the laboratory, not within the US electricity marketplace.

THE NRC MUST BE REFORMED

Nuclear power plants are inherently dangerous. If nuclear power is to play an expanded role in the future, it is imperative that the Nuclear Regulatory Commission become a consistently effective regulator. UCS believes that this goal is attainable. The Maintenance Rule (10 CFR [Code of Federal Regulations] 50.63) and the revised reactor oversight process demonstrate that the agency is capable of effective regulation. That capability must be extended across all of the NRC's oversight functions and consistently sustained. This transformation may require that the agency receive additional resources, particularly during the transformation phase. Because the agency is currently a fee-based agency, it may require legislative changes to supplement the existing resources with taxpayer money.

Failing to reform the Nuclear Regulatory Commission could have tragic consequences. As reported in *The Wall Street Journal*, the 1986 accident at the Chernobyl nuclear plant cost the former Soviet Union several times the net benefits from all Soviet reactors ever operated. The price tag for the accident was placed at 170 to 215 billion rubles while the net benefits from every Soviet nuclear power plant was only 10 to 50 billion rubles. With the price of failure so very high, it is absolutely imperative that the Nuclear Regulatory Commission be a consistently—rather than occasionally—effective regulator.

If Congress wants an expanded role for nuclear power, it must provide the NRC with the resources needed for the agency to implement consistently effective regulatory programs and must also oversee the agency's reform efforts to verify that they are successful.

Radioactive Terrorism: Inadequate Plant Security Must Be Updated

DANIEL HIRSCH

Following the terrorist attacks on September 11, 2001, the Nuclear Regulatory Commission (NRC) first issued a statement that declared U.S. nuclear reactor containments able to withstand a similar crash of a fully loaded jumbo jet. Days later, the NRC retracted its initial statement and acknowledged that current nuclear power plant design could not endure such a crash. After this revelation, Daniel Hirsch, president of the Committee to Bridge the Gap, a Los Angeles–based nuclear policy organization, built his case against the laxity of the NRC and its outdated security regulations.

The NRC requires plants to undergo surprise attack scenarios that consist of one team: three external attackers and one insider. In contrast, plants must provide only a minimum of five guards. Hirsch notes that the details of the September 11 terrorist plot reveal the gross inadequacy of these requirements. Troubled by a lack of response from the government and a return to business as usual, Hirsch laments that such political and economic concerns outweigh the value of human life.

The question immediately arose on September 11, and has persisted: As horrific as the terrorist attacks were, what might have happened if the terrorists who seized jumbo jets and used them as weapons against the World Trade Center and the Pentagon had aimed them at nuclear power plants instead? And if more attacks are likely, as government officials have said, are nuclear facilities on the terrorist target list?

The *Sunday Times* of London reported in October [2001] that some intelligence assessments suggest that the intended target of the fourth plane, the one downed in Pennsylvania, was a nuclear power reactor. The plane had descended much too soon for Washington to be its intended destination, these assessments indicate, suggesting that the true target may have been one of several nuclear plants in its flight path, with the single still-operating unit at Three Mile Island seeming the most likely. This assessment cannot be confirmed, of course. But if it is correct, we owe even more to those brave passengers who succeeded, at the cost of their own lives, in bringing the plane down before it reached its intended target.

MISLEADING STATEMENTS ABOUT PLANT DESIGN

Immediately after the September 11 attacks, the U.S. Nuclear Regulatory Commission (NRC) and the nuclear industry issued statements asserting that U.S. reactor containments were designed to withstand the crash of a fully loaded jumbo jet. Within days, both had to recant and admit that the opposite was the case. Just hours after the terrorist attacks, NRC spokesperson Breck Henderson said U.S. nuclear plants were safe because "containment structures are designed to withstand the impact of a 747."

Ten days later he admitted that "the initial cut we had on that was misleading." In a formal statement, the agency conceded that it "did not specifically contemplate attacks by aircraft such as Boeing 757s and 767s, and nuclear power plants were not designed to withstand such crashes." A similar pattern of assurance followed by retraction characterized the behavior of public relations personnel for a number of specific nuclear sites.

Early on, however, David Kyd, spokesperson for the International Atomic Energy Agency (IAEA), was quoted as saying that most nuclear plants, built during the 1960s and 1970s, were designed to withstand only accidental, glancing impacts from the smaller aircraft used at the time. "If you postulate the risk of a jumbo jet full of fuel, it is clear that their design was not conceived to withstand such an impact," he said. In reporting Kyd's comments, the Associated Press quoted an unnamed U.S. government official to the effect that a direct hit at high speed by a modern jumbo jet "could create a Chernobyl situation."

The press has focused on the vulnerability of reactor containment buildings to airborne attack. But there are also "soft targets" outside containment, and their protection is critical to preventing radioactive release. Excessive emphasis on the risk of air attack obscures the far larger and more frightening possibility of ground assault or the threat from insiders. Security at the nation's nuclear plants has been grossly inadequate for decades, and the nuclear industry and its captive regulatory agency, the NRC, have refused to do anything about it—both before and after September 11.

THE DEVASTATING EFFECTS OF A PLANT MELTDOWN

A typical nuclear power plant contains within its core about 1,000 times the long-lived radioactivity released by the Hiroshima bomb. The spent fuel pools at nuclear power plants typically contain some multiple of that—several Chernobyls' worth.

Any analogy with the dropping of a bomb is imperfect, of course, because much of the destruction caused by an atomic bomb comes from blast effects, and the damage caused by a terrorist attack on a nuclear plant would stem almost exclusively from the release of radioactivity. However, the potential casualties from an atomic attack and those resulting from using conventional explosives to produce a radiological release from a nuclear facility would be surprisingly similar. For example, the NRC estimated years ago that a meltdown at one of the San Onofre reactors in Southern California could produce 130,000 "prompt" fatalities, 300,000 latent cancers, and 600,000 genetic defects. Analyses for other reactors performed by Sandia National Laboratories for the NRC estimated damages up to $314 billion in 1980 dollars (the equivalent of about $700 billion today).

Because there is an immense amount of radioactivity at a reactor, and because the fuel must be constantly cooled to prevent it from melting and releasing that radioactivity, it is not difficult to understand why nuclear facilities might be a tempting target. As Bennett Ramberg pointed out in 1984 in his seminal book on the subject, *Nuclear Power Plants as Weapons for the Enemy: An Unrecognized Military Peril,* any country that possesses nuclear energy facilities gives its adversaries a quasi-nuclear capability to use against it. Conventional explosives—a truck bomb, for example—could cause a massive radiological release, with terrorists turning their adversaries' own technology against them. And just as simple box-cutters were used to convert U.S. jumbo jets into guided missiles, conventional means could turn U.S. nuclear plants into radiological weapons. The need to protect nuclear facilities against terrorist attack should be obvious.

SECURITY REGULATIONS ARE OUTDATED

Yet for decades, NRC regulations have required only minimal security. Fifteen years ago in the March 1986 *Bulletin* ("Protecting Reactors from Terrorists"), two colleagues and I warned even then that terrorist trends were rendering the NRC security rules inadequate. But with only a single, partial exception, the agency's primary security regulations are unchanged from a quarter century ago. And despite September 11—when the NRC's assumptions crumbled at the moment the Twin Towers fell—both the industry and the agency that regulates it continue to resist making any significant improvement to dismally inadequate and outmoded security regulations.

We reported in 1986—and it is still the case today—that NRC regulations require nuclear reactor operators to protect against no more than a single insider and/or three external attackers, acting as a single team, wielding no more than hand-held automatic weapons.

Security personnel at power reactors are not required to be prepared for:

- more than three intruders;
- more than one team of attackers using coordinated tactics;
- more than one insider;
- weapons greater than hand-held automatic weapons;
- attack by boat or plane; or
- any attack by "enemies of the United States," whether governments or individuals.

For years, reactor sites were not even required to provide protection against truck bombs. But after a decade of efforts by the Committee to Bridge the Gap and the Nuclear Control Institute to get the agency to strengthen security and repeated refusals by the NRC to require greater protection, the 1993 World Trade Center bombing and an intrusion event at Three Mile Island finally propelled the agency to amend the rules. But the truck bomb rule is still a concern because of the limited size of the explosion that operators must protect against. It apparently requires protection against truck bombs of roughly the size used at the World Trade Center in 1993, but not the larger quantities of explosives that have been used in similar attacks since then. The NRC is behind the curve, "fighting the last war" rather than protecting against threats that can materialize without warning.

To deal with the limited threat that the NRC does recognize—called the "design basis threat" (DBT)—the agency requires a nuclear power plant to be guarded by a total of five individuals. It may seem incomprehensible in today's world that targets capable of producing tens or hundreds of thousands of casualties and hundreds of billions of dollars of damage are protected by a mere five guards, but that is the minimum the NRC mandates.

The events of September 11 demonstrated the inadequacy

of the agency's quarter-century-old security rules. There were 19 terrorists on the planes, and possibly additional participants in the conspiracy—far in excess of the three external attackers the NRC envisages. They acted as four coordinated teams, but the NRC rule requires the nuclear industry to guard against only a single team. They used jumbo jets filled with jet fuel as their weapons, far more lethal than the hand-carried automatic weapons and explosives contemplated in the regulation. They were very sophisticated, training for months to fly big jets, and willing to die—a level of motivation and capability far beyond that upon which the NRC rules are predicated.

None of the details of the agency's DBT are secret. With a single exception discussed below, they can all be found in the Code of Federal Regulations, available in most libraries and on the Internet. Any potential adversary can immediately learn that the required security arrangements that protect these high-value targets are inadequate.

THE NRC REQUIRES PREPARATION FOR LIMITED THREATS ONLY

The only aspect of the DBT that is not explicitly stated in the Code is the famous number "three"—the maximum number of external attackers against which reactor owners must provide protection. The Code indicates that reactors must be protected against an attack by "several" intruders, and that "several" is less than the number required to operate as more than one team. This is enough to give a pretty clear indication of exactly how small the DBT is, but other publicly available documents make it clear that "several" means three.

The number was publicly revealed as a consequence of the licensing hearings for the Diablo Canyon nuclear plant in California in the early 1980s. The Governor of California was a party in the hearings, in which the adequacy of security at the plant was a key issue. The state's security experts testified that a dozen attackers was a credible number to safeguard against. But the utility, Pacific Gas & Electric (PG&E), and the NRC staff argued that irrespective of any threat that might exist,

NRC requirements were far more modest. The precise number in the DBT became a key issue in the hearings.

The NRC's Atomic Safety and Licensing Appeal Board decided in favor of PG&E and the NRC staff, expressly ruling on how many attackers a reactor operator is required to protect against. The ruling was not immediately published on the theory that it contained sensitive information. The specific number for the DBT, according to the Diablo decision, was withdrawn at the last minute from the published regulations and replaced with "several," not for any security reason, but because the commission thought it would have trouble explaining to the public why it was requiring a lesser level of protection against sabotage for reactors than against theft at non-reactor sites. This remains the case today—NRC nervousness about public discussion of the DBT of three external attackers is not motivated by a security concern, but by fear of embarrassment were it widely known that it only required reactors be capable of protecting against no more than a trivial terrorist challenge.

The Governor of California, however, asked that an expurgated version of the decision be published, and the agency agreed. When the "sanitized" Appeal Board decision was released, the actual number had been deleted. But ironically, the remaining text explained what "several" meant, and other underlying documents cited in the text—which had been publicly released—gave away the actual number.

The Appeal Board ruling cited a number of NRC documents it relied on in concluding that the DBT should be limited to three attackers. And although the ruling was redacted, all of the underlying documents were available in the NRC's public reading room. Those documents, the "SECY [Office of the Secretary] Memoranda," are the agency's actual decision documents on adopting the rule. Over and over again the SECY Memoranda state that the DBT in the rule is "an external threat of one to three persons armed with pistols, shotguns, or rifles (including automatic weapons), and who may be assisted by an insider (employee or unescorted person)."

This is the so-called "three-and-one" threat described in publicly available NRC documents.

The Appeal Board decision discloses some of the rationale for settling on three external attackers. First, the board states, power plants by rule are not required to protect against more than one team of attackers—only fuel-cycle facilities with weapons-grade material must do that. Because the minimum number of attackers who could operate as more than one team is obviously four, three is the maximum number of attackers who cannot act as more than one team.

ONLY A MINIMUM OF FIVE GUARDS IS MANDATORY

Second, and perhaps most astonishingly, the Appeal Board discloses how the regulation's minimum force of five guards was derived:

> "A response force ratio (i.e., ratio of guards to attackers) must be equal to 1 [1 to 1] to protect power reactors. The report [the NRC staff report that formed the basis for the numerical determination for the design basis threat] then states: 'Given the above response force ratio *modified by a measure of conservatism,* the minimum number of guards available for response to an assault may be determined. Therefore, for the presently specified threat, the minimum number of guards available for response at a nuclear power plant is judged to be 5'" (emphasis added).

The Appeal Board decision went on to indicate that the "presently specified threat" referred to was the external threat (of three) along with a single insider capable of participating in a violent attack. This three-and-one threat created a maximum total of four attackers. A 1:1 ratio of guards to attackers would require only four guards. But modifying the ratio "by a measure of conservatism" (giving the guards a one-person advantage) resulted in the regulations requiring a minimum of five guards.

(The actual regulation mentions a "nominal" number of 10 guards, with a minimum of five. But the Diablo decision and underlying documents indicate that this "nominal" number was employed to "camouflag[e] the exact threat.")

Thus, the NRC security regulations, unchanged except to require protection against small-sized truck bombs, require operators to protect against an attack by three outsiders, perhaps aided by one insider, with no team-maneuvering tactics, no attack by boat or air, and minimal hand-held weapons.

This rule made little sense when it was first adopted, and it makes even less today. The September 11 attacks—with at least 19 attackers, four times as many teams, and a level of sophistication far beyond that contemplated by the agency—blew away the NRC's security regulations. Yet those regulations remain unchanged.

THE CONCERNS OF NUCLEAR POLICY ANALYSTS FALL ON DEAF EARS

For 17 years, my group, the Committee to Bridge the Gap, joined by the Nuclear Control Institute, has worked quietly behind the scenes in a largely futile effort to convince the NRC to upgrade its security requirements. With one partial exception, the truck bomb rule, we have failed.

In 1984, in the wake of truck bombings in the Middle East, the NRC staff decided to consider requiring protection against truck bombs at U.S. power reactors. It commissioned Sandia National Laboratories to study the vulnerability of plants to truck bomb attacks. The results were frightening—small truck bombs could cause "unacceptable damage to vital reactor systems," and larger truck bombs could have the same effect, even if detonated off site, because the exclusion zone surrounding many facilities is small. Inexplicably, after the study was conducted, the agency dropped the idea of a truck bomb rule.

In 1985, the Committee to Bridge the Gap testified before the Safeguards and Security Subcommittee of the NRC Advisory Committee on Reactor Safeguards, pointing to data showing increasing terrorist capabilities and actions, urging the agency to upgrade the regulations to deal with larger attacking forces and with truck bombs. The response was unenthusiastic, with many subcommittee members indicating that there were so many ways to destroy a reactor that, if you protected against truck bombs, you'd have to protect against all those other vulnerabilities as well.

Over the next few years, both the Committee to Bridge the Gap and the Nuclear Control Institute continued to push the NRC to upgrade security regulations, to no avail. In 1991, at the time of the war with Iraq and the prospect of terrorist attacks against U.S. targets, we formally petitioned the NRC to upgrade its regulations. In addition to urging protection against truck bombs, the petition called for a new DBT with 20 external attackers (ironic in light of the 19 terrorists on the planes on September 11) capable of operating as two or more teams, with weapons and explosives more significant than hand-held rifles. The NRC denied the petition, ruling that "there has been no change in the domestic threat since the design basis threat was adopted that would justify a change."

Finally, after the truck bomb attack on the World Trade Center in 1993 and an event at Three Mile Island in which an intruder drove a station wagon through the perimeter and into the turbine building, where he stayed for hours while security tried to figure out if he had a bomb, the NRC adopted a new rule requiring some measure of protection against truck bombs. However, the rule may not be sufficient to protect against truck bombs of the size that have been used since 1993.

The rest of the DBT remains unaltered, despite the NRC's promises in 1994 that in a second phase it would consider upgrading the rest of the security regulations.

In fact, a number of actions have weakened security. For example, in 1996 the NRC issued Generic Letter 96–02, "Reconsideration of Nuclear Power Plant Security Requirements Associated with an Internal Threat." It permitted "reductions in unnecessary or marginally effective security measures," granting licensees the option, for instance, to keep "doors to vital areas . . . unlocked."

In late 1998, I received a plain manila envelope in the mail. Inside were documents indicating that the NRC had recently terminated its only counterterrorism program, called the Operational Safeguards Response Evaluation program, (OSRE). The program evaluated nuclear plant security by undertaking mock terrorist attacks—"black hat" force-on-force exercises. The documents contained astonishing information: Given six months advance warning, including the date on which the security test would occur, plants prepared by increasing their guard force by as much as 80 percent. Even so, security failed the tests. In nearly half of the tests conducted at the country's reactors, mock terrorists penetrated security and reached at least one "target set" that, had the intruders been actual terrorists, could have resulted in a meltdown and massive radioactivity release.

This failure rate is extraordinary. No terrorist group is going to give notice six months in advance of when and where it intends to attack. And these tests were against the existing DBT—against only three intruders.

Other publicly available NRC documents from the early 1990s indicate that in an OSRE test at the Peach Bottom reactor, it took only 17 seconds for the mock terrorists to penetrate the perimeter fence and breach the access control barrier. It took intruders 18 seconds at San Onofre, 30 seconds at Duane Arnold, and 45 seconds at Maine Yankee.

And what was the response to this dismal failure rate? The NRC killed the program—there could be no more failures if there were no more tests.

My organization passed the OSRE documents along to the *Los Angeles Times,* which ran a major story about the program's termination. The agency was sufficiently embarrassed that a couple of days later Shirley Jackson, then NRC chair, reinstated the program. Since then, however, the industry and the agency have worked together to gut the tests. Earlier this year, the NRC approved the industry's proposed self-evaluation program that would replace NRC-run force-on-force tests. Companies failing the independent tests are now able to test themselves! The problems inherent in self-regulation should be obvious.

AFTER SEPTEMBER 11: BUSINESS AS USUAL

Our two organizations have persisted in so-far-fruitless attempts to get the DBT upgraded. Last year, we met with NRC Chairman Richard Meserve, trying once again to get the NRC to fix gaping security problems. Nothing came of the meeting. As we were leaving, Meserve said we should feel free to see him again, adding something to the effect that he meets with industry "all the time," and there is no reason he can't meet with public groups from time to time as well. (And indeed, as we left we saw a number of industry lobbyists sitting outside his office waiting to go in.)

After September 11, we wrote to Chairman Meserve, urging him to recommend that the National Guard be called out to protect all the nation's reactors, that air defenses be deployed to protect them, and that employees and contractor personnel be thoroughly re-vetted.

We also asked the NRC to upgrade its security regulations immediately to protect against attacks involving greater numbers, operating as multiple teams, with more than one insider; require a strong two-person rule and other enhanced measures to protect against insiders; require protection against a truck bomb as big as a large truck can carry; require protections against boat and airplane attacks; require full security protection of spent fuel storage pools and dry cask storage, including after reactor closure; and that the Operational Safeguards Response Evaluation program be reinstated and expanded.

The NRC response was business as usual. The agency is continually reviewing the DBT, we were told, just as we have been told for the last 17 years.

But no improvements were promised and none has been made. Both the Committee to Bridge the Gap and the Nuclear Control Institute have decided that after years of quiet work it is time to go public about these problems. It is clear that the United States has sophisticated adversaries out there and everything we know is available to them as well. The only people not taking the danger seriously are the ones who should be required to do something about it—the nuclear industry and the agency that is supposed to regulate it.

All the NRC has done in the wake of the attacks on the World Trade Center and the Pentagon is to recommend—not even require—that licensees go to a higher state of alert within their existing security system and within the existing DBT. A no-fly-zone excluded small planes from flying near power reactors, but after a week that restriction was lifted. The federal government has failed to call out the National Guard—although in the absence of federal action, some governors have taken that step on their own. The NRC and the industry strongly oppose legislation introduced by Sens. Harry Reid, Hillary Clinton, Jim Jeffords, Joe Lieberman, and Cong. Ed Markey that would have required the agency to upgrade security regulations.

RESCUING THE NRC—AND OURSELVES— FROM THE INDUSTRY IT SHOULD BE REGULATING

In 1981, the NRC and industry argued against the Governor of California's contention in the Diablo case that there should be protection against up to a dozen terrorists, saying such an attack wasn't credible. In 1991, the NRC and industry argued against our rulemaking petition that the DBT be increased from three to 20 external attackers operating as several teams, again asserting that there was no evidence there could ever be an attack of more than three as a single team. Protections against attacks by boats, large truck bombs, or from the air remain beyond the design threat. On September 11, 19 attackers in four teams using planes caused the worst terrorist event in U.S. history. Yet the NRC and industry refuse to upgrade the DBT regulations to a level consistent with the now-evident threat.

The industry's response is shocking. Rather than conceding the vulnerability of its facilities and the need to upgrade security, at a press conference on September 25 a spokesman for the Nuclear Energy Institute took the extraordinary stand that greater security isn't required because Chernobyl wasn't that bad.

Why does the industry continue to ignore the need to protect its facilities? First, more security means more expense, and its every instinct is to avoid current expenses. Second, if it admits its reactors are vulnerable, the industry's dream of a nuclear renaissance is diminished.

Having received a big boost from the [Vice President Dick] Cheney energy plan, the industry had been hoping to build new reactors, supposedly of the new pebble-bed design. In order to save money, these "passively safe" reactors would be built without a containment structure. In addition, they are made of graphite, which burns readily, as evidenced by Chernobyl and the earlier Windscale accident in Britain. As poorly resistant to terrorism as today's reactors are, pebble-bed reactors would be far worse. Furthermore, the industry-Cheney proposals involve a revival of the idea of reprocessing spent fuel to separate plutonium, which would then be used in civil reactors, creating a massive additional risk that terrorists might acquire nuclear weapons materials from poorly guarded civilian power plants. The nuclear industry hopes that its post–September 11 problems will go away, without having to upgrade security.

And why has the NRC not imposed upgraded security requirements? Put bluntly, the NRC is arguably the most captured regulatory agency in the federal government, a creature of the industry it is intended to regulate. Efforts to separate its promotional and regulatory functions, which led to the breakup of the Atomic Energy Commission in the mid-1970s, have failed utterly. The NRC's principal interest is in assisting the industry, keeping regulatory burdens and expenses to a bare minimum, and helping to jumpstart the nuclear enterprise.

But the risk of terrorist attack at one or more nuclear plants is simply too great to allow this failed agency and the industry it allegedly regulates to continue to ignore the need to provide reasonable protection. The industry's short-term economic or political concerns pale in comparison to the damage that would occur if attackers turn the nation's reactors into radiological weapons.

CHAPTER 4

THE MOVEMENT TODAY: THE CAUSE REMAINS ACTIVE

AMERICAN
SOCIAL
MOVEMENTS

Ending the New Arms Race Before It Begins

DARYL G. KIMBALL

"There are tons of weapons-grade fissionable material and thousands of warheads now sitting in Russian facilities that are less secure than many American homes." With that opinion, peace activist Daryl G. Kimball begins his exploration of the nuclear dangers threatening our world today. Nuclear terrorism, obsolete Cold War postures of U.S. and Russian nuclear forces, and waning international deterrence are contributing to the creation of a new, destabilizing arms race, he argues. Kimball believes the only solution is the eventual elimination of all nuclear weapons.

Kimball is the former executive director of the Coalition to Reduce Nuclear Dangers, an alliance of international arms control and disarmament groups working toward a program to reduce nuclear dangers worldwide and prevent new threats from developing. He is currently the executive director of the Arms Control Association.

I n the movie, *The Peacemaker* [1997], the ultimate nuclear terrorist threat is played out: a well-organized and well-financed terrorist group boards a military train loaded with Russian nuclear weapons and escapes with SS-18 warheads, one of which is smuggled into the United States for an attack on New York City. The movie indulges in some Hollywood-style hyperbole, but the plot line is not far removed from well-documented, real-life incidents.

At least 20 times each year since 1992, Russian or Western authorities have apprehended individuals with stolen nuclear

Excerpted from "Ending Nuclear Terror," by Daryl G. Kimball, www.clw.org, Winter 1998. Copyright © 1998 by Council for a Livable World. Reprinted with permission.

materials. At a highway rest stop in Germany, in a restaurant in the Czech Republic, and on the Turkish border, nuclear thieves have been arrested at the last moment while trying to sell their smuggled materials. For those thieves not apprehended, an eager market awaits. There is evidence that certain nations and groups, including known terrorist organizations, are attempting to acquire Soviet nuclear materials from inside the former Soviet Union.

The consequences, should they succeed, would be catastrophic. As Senator Richard Lugar (R-IN) warned in 1995:

> Suppose that instead of mini-vans filled with hundreds of pounds of the crude explosives used in Oklahoma City and New York [World Trade Center], terrorists had acquired a suitcase carrying a grapefruit-sized 100 pounds of highly-enriched uranium. Assuming a simple, well-known design, a weapon fashioned from this material would produce a nuclear blast equivalent to 10,000 to 20,000 tons of TNT. Under normal conditions, this would devastate a three-square-mile urban area. Most of the people of Oklahoma City would have disappeared. In the case of New York, the tip of Manhattan, including all the Wall Street financial district, would have been destroyed.

A CRISIS IN RUSSIA RAISES AWARENESS IN THE UNITED STATES

The risk of theft, sale or diversion of nuclear materials from Russia's military research and production complex has increased as the facilities, once the best-funded in the Soviet Union, struggle to pay their staffs, assure adequate security, and maintain proper accounting of all their nuclear materials. There are tons of weapons-grade fissionable material and thousands of warheads now sitting in Russian facilities that are less secure than many American homes.

In February 1997, the institute responsible for designing the sophisticated control systems for Russia's Strategic Nuclear Rocket Forces staged a one-day strike to protest pay arrears and the lack of resources to upgrade their equipment. Three days later, the Russian Defense Minister Igor Rodinov said that "if the shortage of funds persists . . . Russia may soon approach a threshold beyond which its missile and nuclear systems become uncontrollable." Reports from the Central Intelligence Agency confirm that Russia's Strategic Rocket Forces are not immune to the growing lack of discipline and resources that also plague Russia's conventional armed forces.

Fortunately, a bipartisan group of U.S. policy-makers has had the vision to put together a new line of defense to eliminate these threats at their source. The current U.S. nuclear threat reduction policy, termed the Cooperative Threat Reduction (CTR) program, is a combination of programs that grew out of legislation originally sponsored by Senators Sam Nunn (D-GA) and Richard Lugar (R-IN) in 1991. These programs now encompass several goals:

- Destroy the nuclear weapons delivery systems which once threatened the West;
- Safely transport the warheads from the deployment sites to areas where they will be dismantled;
- Create safeguards against proliferation and the spread of the scientific knowledge that built the Soviet nuclear arsenal;
- Improve nuclear materials control by upgrading security at Russian nuclear installations and installing modern accounting and inventory practices; and
- Assist in defense conversion efforts.

After a slow start, the Nunn-Lugar program, now in its sixth year, is producing measurable national security gains. Thousands of missiles that were once aimed at American cities and military targets have been dismantled and stored, thousands of once disaffected nuclear weapons scientists are employed on civilian projects, and dozens of nuclear facilities have been made more secure. Nuclear terrorism, however, is just part of a larger, continuing threat posed by nuclear weapons.

In the early morning hours of January 25, 1995, Norway launched a weather research rocket. There was nothing unusual about the launch. Russian authorities had been notified well in advance. Unfortunately, bureaucratic snafus within the Russian apparatus prevented the proper notification of all appropriate personnel.

Shortly after the rocket's launch, a troubling blip suddenly appeared on the screens at radar stations across Russia's northern frontier. The station technicians had reason to be concerned: a single U.S submarine-launched ballistic missile can scatter eight, 475 kiloton nuclear bombs over Moscow within fifteen minutes. They immediately alerted their superiors, who forwarded the message to a just wakened President Boris Yeltsin. With just minutes to react, Yeltsin, with Russia's suitcase of nuclear launch control orders beside him, discussed options with his top advisors. For the first time ever, the "suitcase" was activated as radar operators continued to monitor the trajectory of the unknown missile. Eight minutes into the crisis, just moments before Russian nuclear weapons would have to be launched to respond to an impending attack, it was finally determined that the "missile" was headed away from Russia and out over the sea. A near disaster had been averted.

Despite the Cold War's end and significant decreases in nuclear arsenals since the mid-1980s, the nuclear force postures of the United States and Russia remain fundamentally the same: each side maintains thousands of strategic nuclear weapons that are maintained on "hair-trigger" alert, awaiting a warning of oncoming attack from the other side. Because most nuclear weapons systems are designed to be launched within minutes notice, each side still depends on the accuracy and proper interpretation of the data from early warning radars. Although Presidents [Bill] Clinton and Yeltsin . . . announced that weapons have been "de-targeted" to try to send accidentally launched intercontinental nuclear missiles into the oceans rather than into each others' cities, these nuclear weapons systems can be re-targeted within minutes.

The threat of a massive nuclear war and the death and injury of hundreds of millions of people still haunts our civilization. Between them, the United States and Russia are still capable of launching approximately 5,000 nuclear warheads at each others' cities within a half hour. As a recent National Academy of Sciences report, entitled *The Future of U.S. Nuclear Weapons Policy,* concluded, the result of these policies is that "the risks posed by nuclear weapons remain unacceptably high.". . .

WEAPONS ENCOURAGE WAR, NOT DETER IT

When the Soviets attempted to place nuclear weapons on Cuban soil in the early 1960s, we came the closest we have ever come to a nuclear exchange. But in this case nuclear weapons did not deter the threat, they created it. The Soviets, in attempting to deploy medium-range nuclear weapons in Cuba, were responding to a similar deployment of U.S. medium-range missiles in Turkey. Moreover, as is illustrated in the . . . published volume, *The Kennedy Tapes: Inside the White House During the Cuban Missile Crisis,* it was as much good luck as good management that nuclear weapons were not used during the incident. In the early days of the crisis, the U.S. military was strongly urging Kennedy to invade Cuba and eliminate the missiles by force. Had this occurred, we now know that the already operational missiles might have been fired to avoid their destruction. In the end, Kennedy chose a naval blockade, which itself risked a conflict with nuclear consequences. Thus, nuclear weapons have not, in and of themselves, prevented a direct superpower conflict. Instead, they exponentially increased the scale of destruction if such a conflict occurred.

Even if one accepts the dubious argument that nuclear weapons were needed during the Cold War, however, that need has now disappeared. The collapse of the Soviet Union has substantially changed the political and military relationship between the superpowers that drove the nuclear arms race for forty years. Today, with the United States' overwhelming conventional military superiority and ability to project its forces around the world, the only military purpose of maintaining these nuclear stockpiles is to deter the use of nuclear weapons by another country. If nuclear weapons can be substantially reduced or eliminated altogether, so too will any legitimate purpose for their continued existence.

It is also important to realize that today's "new" threat—a terrorist attack involving conventional, chemical, or nuclear devices—cannot be deterred or effectively countered with nuclear weapons. Intercontinental ballistic missiles can do nothing to stop determined terrorists from trying to attack targets with hidden bombs carried on small trucks or in suitcases. Should nuclear devices fall into the hands of such non-governmental actors, the concept of great power nuclear deterrence becomes largely irrelevant.

THE RISK OF A NEW, DESTABILIZING ARMS RACE

While the deterrent value of nuclear weapons has faded along with the end of the Cold War, their dangers still loom large. Terrorism is but one worry. As the Cuban missile crisis and the 1995 Norwegian rocket scare illustrate, the very existence and continued Cold War state of nuclear readiness threatens to lead to the use of nuclear weapons by technical failure, human error, or unauthorized launch.

On these fronts, time is our enemy. The longer we maintain the current nuclear status quo, the higher the likelihood that such factors will lead to disaster. But time is also working against us in other ways.

Despite the success of the existing nuclear non-proliferation regime and especially the 1968 Nuclear Non-Proliferation Treaty (NPT) in preventing several nations from joining the nuclear weapons "club," several states have made progress through clandestine efforts toward the development of nuclear arsenals. While unfortunate, these activities are a natural outgrowth of the nuclear status quo. Possession of nuclear weapons by some states stimulates other nations to acquire them, reducing the security of all. Should the size of the nuclear club grow by even one beyond the present roster of eight (United States, Russia, the United Kingdom, France, China, India, Israel, and Pakistan), the risk of a new and destabilizing arms race may become reality.

Some argue that the United States should retain its nuclear

weapons for this very reason. But this path leads only to a dangerous and unstable chain of events: should the United States and other nuclear weapons powers choose to retain (or even, perhaps, expand) their nuclear weapons stockpiles, other states will seek and, over time, acquire nuclear weapons. The key to breaking this vicious cycle is for existing nuclear states to take steps that de-legitimize nuclear weapons and reaffirm their commitment, already embodied in the Nuclear Non-Proliferation Treaty, to ultimately eliminating them.

Finally, it is important to consider the costs of nuclear weapons during the course of the last five decades—in monetary, environmental and human terms. According to the Brookings Institution's *Nuclear Weapons Cost Study Project,* the U.S. has spent about $4 trillion for its nuclear arsenal since 1940. [As of 1998], the U.S. spends about $24 billion annually on the maintenance, improvement, and operation of its nuclear arsenal. In addition, the environmental legacy of the Cold War—the radioactive and hazardous waste pollution at dozens of nuclear bomb plants—will cost the federal governments in excess of $235 billion over the next 75 years to contain and remediate. And it is impossible to calculate the price paid by the 250,000 atomic veterans exposed to radiation in military exercises and the hundreds of thousands of other Americans exposed to radiation from the bomb plants and the fallout from over 100 atmospheric nuclear weapons tests. Contrary to their "more bang for the buck" label, nuclear weapons have cost the United States dearly.

THE SOLUTION: THE ABOLITION OF NUCLEAR WEAPONS

The end of the Cold War has created an unprecedented opportunity—indeed, a moral imperative—to pursue the elimination of nuclear weapons. Achieving this objective, however, will require the development of effective verification measures. Some critics argue that eliminating nuclear weapons is implausible because developing a perfect, 100 percent certain verification regime would be impossible. Absent total assurance against cheating by any individual state, the nuclear powers will not wish to divest themselves of nuclear weapons entirely.

Such verification measures, however, are not an impossible dream. Some of the most critical components have been put in place already. [On August 16, 1997,] existing international and U.S. verification measures were used to determine that a seismic event near Novaya Zemlya, a Russian island near the Arctic Circle, was in fact an earthquake and not a Russian nuclear test, as was originally suspected. The event was first detected at one of over 300 nuclear monitoring sites already established throughout the world to detect such disturbances. The information was quickly relayed to a data center established by the Pentagon in Arlington, Virginia where it was determined that the event was actually an earthquake that had occurred 80 miles at sea. An Air Force plane was then sent downwind of the site to detect signs of radiation and found nothing. The CIA also engaged its intelligence assets, again confirming that no test had occurred.

Monitoring practices put in place by past arms control agreements complement these technologies and resources. On-site inspections are the ultimate verification tool, supplementing monitoring by satellites, seismometers, infrasound, radioactive gas detectors, and other technologies. Moreover, the very nature of the nuclear weapon scientific-industrial complex—a tightly regimented governmental enterprise with extensive records and information on nuclear weapons and nuclear material—helps verification efforts further still.

Those who doubt that nuclear weapons elimination can be verified base their arguments on the limitations of current technologies and methods. Such technologies and methods may not be perfect, but significant progress is being made. And it is important to remember that nuclear disarmament is an ongoing process that can and will be achieved in stages. It is too early to judge the adequacy of a future nuclear weapons elimination verification regime that will not be developed for some time. In the meantime, current and pending arms control agreements—including SALT [Strategic Arms Limitation Talks],

START [Strategic Arms Reduction Talks], INF [Intermediate-Range Nuclear Forces Treaty], CFE [Conventional Forces in Europe Treaty] and CWC [Chemical Weapons Convention]—provide strong evidence of our ability to improve and advance verification measures with each step forward.

Finally, if some risks must be taken to achieve complete abolition, they should be compared to those already posed by the continued operational deployment of thousands of nuclear weapons worldwide. In the meantime, the uncertainties that surround verification should not be allowed to divert attention from practical intermediate steps to reduce existing nuclear dangers.

Practical Steps to Reduce and Eliminate Nuclear Dangers

For these and other reasons, a growing number of national security specialists, former military commanders, research institutions and leading political figures are urging new steps to address the nuclear danger. In December 1996, General George Lee Butler (retired), former Chief of the U.S. Strategic Command with responsibility for all U.S. nuclear forces under President [George H.W.] Bush, along with 60 other former U.S. and foreign military leaders, issued a call to eliminate all nuclear weapons. Former Senator Sam Nunn has called for immediate action to reduce nuclear force alert levels to help prevent the possibility of accidental or unauthorized launch. The 1996 report of the Canberra Commission on the Elimination of Nuclear Weapons, which included military and political leaders from the nuclear weapons states, as well as leading non-nuclear states, proposed a series of steps that could lead to the elimination of nuclear weapons.

These and other leaders and experts are now advocating that the United States, Russia, and the other declared and undeclared nuclear weapon states act quickly on a series of practical, achievable measures to immediately reduce the nuclear threat. The following near-term initiatives are common to most of these recent proposals:

- *Ratify and implement the Comprehensive Nuclear Test Ban Treaty (CTBT)*. The CTBT would ban all nuclear test explosions and severely impede the development of sophisticated new types of nuclear weapons. In doing so this ban would help constrain nuclear weapons proliferation, guard against a new arms race between the existing nuclear weapon states, and reinforce the nuclear nonproliferation regime. Because the United States does not have any plans or needs to produce new types of nuclear weapons, and because the existing stockpile can be maintained effectively without testing, nuclear testing is no longer necessary to maintain U.S. nuclear capabilities. In September 1997, the Treaty was sent to the Senate for its advice and consent for ratification. A vote is expected by 1998. [As of January 2002, the Treaty remains unratified.]

- *Encourage Russian ratification of the START II agreement and immediately begin negotiations on START III*. When fully implemented the START I and II treaties will reduce the number of U.S. deployed strategic nuclear warheads from 7,150 to 3,500, and the number of Russian warheads from 6,670 to 3,100. To encourage the Russian Duma, the nation's primary legislative body, to ratify START II [in winter 1998], the U.S. should agree to begin START III negotiations immediately. START III would reduce each country's arsenal to 2,000 to 2,500 warheads and begin a process of irreversible de-activation of those warheads. In addition, each side should agree to begin elimination of their "reserve" warhead stocks, which will continue to represent a "breakout" threat so long as they still exist.

- *Remove from hair-trigger alert nuclear weapons in the U.S. and Russian nuclear arsenals*. Each side could immediately reduce the number of weapons on alert to START III levels (2,000–2,500 strategic warheads) as an interim step, and follow-up measures should be pursued thereafter to take the majority of U.S. and Russian nuclear weapons off continuous alert. Such measures would appreciably reduce the possibility of unauthorized or accidental launch by increasing the time needed to prepare and launch them.

- *Bring China, the United Kingdom, France and the undeclared nuclear weapon states into the nuclear risk reduction process.* As U.S. and Russian deployed nuclear stockpiles approach 1,000 warheads, the other nuclear weapon states should be engaged in nuclear reduction negotiations. The goal should be to reduce each of these nation's nuclear arsenals to 100–200 nuclear warheads.

- *Maintain the Nunn-Lugar Program.* This program, our core response to "loose nukes" and the associated threat of nuclear terrorism, must be maintained. The program has recently been criticized by those who question why U.S. money should be spent in Russia when it has yet to ratify START II. But withholding Nunn-Lugar funds will not convince a recalcitrant Russia into compliance, nor will sticking our head in the sand about Russia's nuclear security problems improve our own security situation. Should nuclear weapons or sufficient fissile material to produce them become available to would-be nuclear weapon states or terrorist organizations, cities like Washington or Oklahoma City—not Moscow or Vladivostok—are the most likely targets. The United States spends billions of dollars each year to deter the use of strategic nuclear weapons held by national governments. At less than $400 million per year, the Nunn-Lugar program is a solid investment producing lasting security dividends.

- *Improve Verifiability.* Improving nuclear security, accounting and transparency of nuclear stockpiles by expanding the Nunn-Lugar program can better prevent the spread of nuclear materials, weapons, and know-how from the former-Soviet Union. If efforts to better control nuclear material inside Russia's warhead dismantlement facilities are not achieved within the next 3–4 years, our opportunity to account for and monitor the nuclear warheads dismantled as a result of U.S.-Russian nuclear arms reduction agreements may be lost.

- *Expand the number of nuclear weapons–free zones.* In 1996, the U.S. signed the Treaty of Rarotonga, which creates a Nuclear Weapons Free Zone (NWFZ) in the South Pacific. As a signatory the U.S. pledges not to use or threaten to use nuclear weapons against any nation party to the Treaty. The U.S. was also an original signer of the Treaty of Pelindaba, which creates an African NWFZ. There are now five NWFZs worldwide, which together cover most of the Southern Hemisphere. An explicit pledge by NATO not to deploy nuclear weapons in the three new NATO member states (Poland, the Czech Republic, and Hungary) would effectively create a non-nuclear buffer zone in Central Europe.

A FLAWED ALTERNATIVE: NATIONAL MISSILE DEFENSES

Some critics argue that rather than dismantling nuclear weapons and curtailing nuclear weapons testing and production, the United States should halt nuclear arms reductions, resume nuclear testing, and build an elaborate and highly-expensive national ballistic missile defense system. But such policies would only maintain the existing and highly-risky nuclear force postures and accelerate the acquisition of nuclear weapons by additional nations.

Particularly dangerous is a proposal before Congress mandating the deployment of a national missile defense (NMD) system—the concept that was dubbed "Star Wars" when it was proposed by President Ronald Reagan in 1983. A system like this would be costly ($60 billion according to some estimates) and could be easily overwhelmed by a number of technically feasible and relatively inexpensive countermeasures, such as decoys and chaff. In addition, the system outlined in the legislation calls for a national missile defense system against limited ballistic missile attacks (reportedly 5–20 warheads without countermeasures). But an accidental or unauthorized launch could easily involve hundreds or even thousands of nuclear warheads and would overwhelm a limited defense. For unauthorized attacks, one of the most likely scenarios would be a launch of 50–200 warheads from a Russian submarine. A national missile defense system would therefore provide little protection against the risk of an accidental or unauthorized nuclear attack from China or Russia, the main rationale used by national missile defense backers to rush toward deployment by 2003. The problem of accidental and unauthorized launches can be better addressed by less expensive, more effective, verifiable measures such as de-alerting. In addition, a national missile defense would provide no protection whatsoever against a nuclear terrorist attack by a small truck- or suitcase-sized bomb.

NOW IS THE TIME TO ACT

Rather than pursue expensive missile defense programs, the United States and Russia should maintain restraints on national missile defenses established by the Anti-Ballistic Missile Treaty, while pursuing research and development to address threats posed by shorter-range missiles, as recommended by the 1997 National Academy of Sciences study group on U.S. nuclear policy.

Now is not the time to stand still, or worse, step backwards. We must take advantage of the opportunity afforded by the end of the Cold War to address the still precarious nuclear standoff between the U.S., Russia, China, and the other nuclear weapon states. Inaction will have disastrous consequences for our personal and national security.

A New Movement
for a New
Millennium

DAVID CORTRIGHT

David Cortright argues, "While the threat of thermonuclear attack on the United States has diminished, the risks of nuclear weapons being used somewhere in the world are probably greater now than at any time in the nuclear age." As the twenty-first century approached, Cortright fortunately saw a new mobilization of grassroots activism responding to such risks, helping to reform the American antinuclear movement and work toward nuclear abolition. However, he believes the United States has a long way to go toward fulfilling its responsibility to end all nuclear threats, which began when it first developed and used the atomic bomb.

Cortright is president of the Fourth Freedom Forum, an organization that discourages armed aggression and advocates the elimination of nuclear and other weapons of mass destruction through enforceable international law. He is also the former executive director of the Committee for a Sane Nuclear Policy, a leading nuclear freeze group from the 1960s to the 1980s, which merged in 1993 with other freeze advocates to become Peace Action. Since the 1990s Cortright has become a leading authority on the use of nonviolent tools—incentives and sanctions—in international peacemaking.

I n our hearts many of us already live in a post–nuclear era. We so yearn to be free of nuclear fear that our imaginations have leaped ahead to the future. With the menacing dangers of the 1980s seemingly past, we no longer even think of the bomb. We want to believe the president when he says that our children really can sleep safely at night.

But troubling realities intrude and shatter our dreams of security. Nuclear tests in India and Pakistan. Israel's formidable nuclear arsenal amidst the cauldron of Middle East tension. Atomic ambitions in Iraq, Iran, and North Korea. Continuing doubts about the security of nuclear weapons in traumatized Russia. While the threat of thermonuclear attack on the United States has diminished, the risks of nuclear weapons being used somewhere in the world are probably greater now than at any time in the nuclear age.

The United States is a major part of this huge problem, with nuclear weapons as the cornerstone of U.S. defense policy. The U.S. nuclear arsenal stands [in 1999] at approximately 15,000 weapons, and even after all currently planned reductions are completed (in the year 2007 or later) the United States will retain some 10,000 nuclear bombs. More ominously, the role of the bomb in U.S. military doctrine has expanded, and the potential uses of nuclear weapons have multiplied. A December 1997 Presidential Decision Directive extended the role of nuclear weapons to permit their use against countries possessing chemical and biological weapons, against nations with "prospective access" to nuclear weapons, and even against "non-state actors." Under this extraordinary but little noticed doctrine, nuclear weapons can now be used against so-called "rogue states" or terrorist groups suspected of possessing weapons of mass destruction. Nuclear weapons, far from fading away, have taken on frightening new roles and seem destined to remain a permanent and increasingly central element of U.S. military strategy.

ONE GOAL: NUCLEAR ABOLITION

In response to these alarming trends, a new citizen's movement for nuclear sanity is emerging. This new movement is avowedly abolitionist in purpose, consciously drawing a moral parallel to the earlier historic struggle against slavery. The new abolition movement is based as much on hope as fear. It sees the end of the Cold War and collapse of the Soviet Union as a golden opportunity—what [writer and nuclear abolitionist] Jonathan Schell has termed "the gift of time"—to achieve a future free of terror and the fear of annihilation. The new movement is motivated by a passionate yearning to escape the untenable moral dilemma of a defense policy predicated on the threat to annihilate tens of millions of innocent people.

Manifestations of this new movement are evident among former officials and prominent experts. The leading voice is that of Gen. Lee Butler, former commander of U.S. nuclear forces, who in December 1996 stunned the arms control community and the political establishment with an eloquent speech at the National Press Club calling for the complete elimination of nuclear weapons. Butler was joined by 60 retired generals and admirals from the United States, Russia, and other countries in an appeal for nuclear abolition. In January 1998 more than 120 world leaders released an additional statement urging abolition. Among the signatories were 52 past or present presidents and prime ministers. Both statements were organized by the State of the World Forum under the direction of former Sen. Alan Cranston, who has played a central role in the emerging nuclear abolition movement. Other recent actions include:

- In July 1996 the International Court of Justice in the Hague declared that the nuclear weapons states have an obligation to negotiate in good faith for nuclear disarmament.
- In August 1996 the prestigious Canberra Commission released a detailed report arguing for a step-by-step process toward the elimination of nuclear weapons.
- In December 1997 the U.N. General Assembly adopted a resolution urging negotiations for a convention to outlaw nuclear weapons.
- Last June [1998] eight nations issued a joint declaration calling for a world free of nuclear weapons.

As welcome as these international efforts may be, they are no substitute for political pressures within the United States. The United States first developed and used the bomb, and it has a special responsibility to end the nuclear threat. If American political leaders can be convinced to support abolition, other nations will follow suit.

GRASSROOTS ACTIVISM MUST DRIVE THE NEW MOVEMENT

Bringing about such a change will require a massive mobilization of grassroots awareness and pressure. However valuable the many elite statements for disarmament, these declarations are not sufficient to overcome the entrenched power of the nuclear establishment. Politicians will not act unless they are pressured to do so by an informed, articulate, and well-organized citizen constituency. Public opinion polls show widespread support for denuclearization, but this sentiment must be turned into active citizen involvement if change is to occur.

Fortunately there are encouraging signs of re-emerging nuclear activism in the United States. Perhaps the most striking manifestation of this new movement is the statement "The Morality of Nuclear Deterrence," organized by Pax Christi USA and signed by nearly 100 U.S. Catholic bishops. Issued in June 1998, the Pax Christi statement challenges the moral and political validity of deterrence in light of the end of the Cold War and the collapse of the Soviet Union. The statement urges the United States and other nuclear weapons states "to enter into a process leading to the complete elimination of these morally offensive weapons." "Nuclear deterrence as a national policy must be condemned as morally abhorrent," the bishops' statement declares. "We urge all to join in taking up the challenge to begin the effort to eliminate nuclear weapons now, rather than relying on them indefinitely."

Other evidence of renewed disarmament activism can be seen at the grassroots level. Dozens of cities and towns have passed resolutions in favor of nuclear abolition. More than 120 people attended the conference "Bottling the Nuclear Genie" in Chicago in October 1998. Some 300 people attended an abolition conference in Cambridge, Massachusetts, in October 1997. One of the most interesting recent actions was the Vermont Walk for Nuclear Abolition, organized in August

1998 by the American Friends Service Committee. The Walk began with an August 15 rally of 200 people in Montpelier and continued for seven days with about 100 people trekking 93 miles to Springfield. Along the way walkers distributed flyers informing local taxpayers how much of their income taxes are spent on nuclear weapons, an amount which in some towns equals half the local municipal budget....

In October 1998 more than 50 people from 25 national and

Challenging the Anti-Ballistic Missile (ABM) Treaty of 1972

For [President George W.] Bush, the apparent Russian decision to accept a shift in the ABM framework could help realize a prime national security goal—the development of missile defenses through an expanded series of antimissile tests the Pentagon plans to start next spring [2002].

Whether Mr. Bush decides to withdraw from the treaty may turn on how destabilizing it might be—particularly given European concerns about the United States acting alone.

In addition, the Russians plainly still view the ABM treaty as useful. [President Vladimir V.] Putin said tonight, "We believe it is an important element of stability in the world."

Mr. Putin has also publicly warned that to destroy the ABM treaty—and by extension the 30-year legacy of arms control accords—poses the risk of inciting nuclear states like India and Pakistan to continue to ignore the proliferation constraints that hang over them.

Patrick E. Tyler, *New York Times*, October 22, 2001.

regional organizations, including [the Christian ministry] So-journers, gathered in Chicago to discuss the creation of a U.S.-based nuclear abolition campaign. The assembled organizers agreed on the need for an abolition campaign and formed an interim coordinating committee to create the necessary decision-making structure and program strategy. Many of the participants expressed enthusiasm for a proposal from Jonathan Schell to build wide public support for a simple resolution, "Resolved: that it should be the policy of the United States government to proceed speedily to a world without nuclear weapons, and to work actively with other governments to achieve this goal by a certain time." Under the Schell plan, peace groups would approach civic organizations of every kind and ask that they ratify the resolution and appoint an on-going committee to work actively for nuclear abolition.

The task of changing U.S. policy will be a long and difficult one, requiring a multiyear campaign of persistent commitment. The post–nuclear age that we yearn to see will not arrive without determined citizen action. The times are ripe for such a movement, though, and the concept of abolition is gaining legitimacy. We have "the gift of time," but there is also a race against time as nuclear storm clouds threaten. Let us seize the opportunity before us to make a new beginning toward a safer and more secure world without nuclear weapons.

Reviving the Movement: Bringing Nuclear Dangers Back into the American Consciousness

JONATHAN SCHELL

In this selection Jonathan Schell—writer, journalist, and professor—provides an overview of the political factors affecting the American antinuclear movement today. Small in numbers but great in spirit, Schell contends that members of the current movement may be facing a new arms race. The George W. Bush administration has withdrawn the United States from the Anti-Ballistic Missile (ABM) Treaty of 1972 and is working on development of a national missile defense (NMD) system—a space-based weapons system much like former President Ronald Reagan's "Star Wars" initiative, aimed at destroying incoming ballistic missiles—much to the dismay of the international community. Additionally, the increased nuclear proliferation in South Asia prompts Schell to conclude that the current nuclear age is running out of control, and that the world's nuclear dilemmas must once again enter the conscious thoughts of Americans.

Schell has become a leading advocate of nuclear abolition within the contemporary antinuclear movement. This current role began with his publication *The Fate of the Earth*, in which Schell explored the horrific effects that a nuclear holocaust would wreak upon the planet. Schell is currently the peace and disarmament correspondent for the political magazine the *Nation*.

Excerpted from "The New Nuclear Danger," by Jonathan Schell, *Nation,* June 25, 2001. Copyright © 2001 by The Nation Company, L.P. Reprinted with permission.

On June 12, 1982, 1 million people assembled in Central Park in New York City to protest the reckless nuclear policies of the Reagan Administration and to call for a nuclear freeze. They never assembled in such numbers again—in part because Reagan reversed course and opened nuclear arms talks with the Soviet Union, and in part because, after [Soviet president] Mikhail Gorbachev came to power, the cold war began to wind down. The day remains in memory as a reminder of how quickly public concern over nuclear annihilation can arise and how quickly it can evaporate. When the cold war finally did end, nuclear weapons pretty much dropped out of the conscious thoughts of most Americans. The weapons themselves, however, remain in existence—some 32,000 strong at last count. Now the policies of a new administration and the rise of fresh nuclear dangers have brought the issue back to awareness. On June 10 [2001] a coalition of groups that calls itself Project Abolition will hold an antinuclear demonstration in Lafayette Park across from the White House. It will be the first major effort of its kind in the capital since the end of the cold war. The precipitating event is the new arms race that is threatened by the Bush Administration's embrace of National Missile Defense (NMD) and the weaponization of space. A million people are not expected. But the protesters hope to make up in staying power what they lack in numbers. Their underlying cause is the abolition of all nuclear arms, and their vow is to stick with it for the duration.

It is no simple matter to take stock of the nuclear predicament in the year 2001. Under the Bush Administration, the nuclear policies of the United States—and of the world—are in a state of greater confusion than at any time since the weapons were invented. Chaos would not be too strong a word to use. In fact, the greatest current danger may lie not in one policy or another but precisely in this confusion, which leaves the world's nuclear actors without any reliable road map for the future. It is nevertheless essential to try to understand at least the broad outlines of the new shape of the predicament. This exercise is complex and riddled with paradox and contradiction, not to mention wishful thinking and sheer fantasy, yet it is unavoidable if either policy or protest is to make sense.

Nuclear danger today has two main sources. The first is the mountain of nuclear arms left over from the cold war. The second is the proliferation of nuclear weapons to new countries. The leftover cold war arsenals are still governed by the policy that prevailed during the cold war, the doctrine of nuclear deterrence, which holds (in its most enlightened version) that the rival great powers are safest when each has the unchallengeable power to annihilate its rival. This way, no one is supposed to try anything, because if anyone does, all will die. [As of 2001] the United States has about 7,200 weapons poised to fire at Russia, and Russia has about 6,000 poised to fire at us, and the continued existence of each nation depends on the reliability of the other's forces, which is doubtful in the extreme in the case of Russia. Deterrence's provocative other name, of course, is mutual assured destruction, or MAD, a reference to the menace of complete annihilation on which the stability of the arrangement rests. MAD's confusing adjunct is arms control, whose aim has been to draw down the preposterous excess of offensive weapons through the Strategic Arms Reduction Talks (START) while suppressing defenses by observance of the Anti-Ballistic Missile (ABM) treaty of 1972, until this year called the "cornerstone of strategic stability" in NATO [North Atlantic Treaty Organization] planning papers. Defenses had to be suppressed because if they ran free they would upset the laboriously negotiated offensive reductions.

MAD, however, is not a creature of the ABM treaty; it is an inescapable condition in a world of large nuclear arsenals, against which no defenses are available. The ABM treaty merely ratifies and codifies this underlying situation, the better to negotiate the reduction—though not the elimination— of offensive forces. Other things being equal, a world without an ABM treaty would not be a world without MAD; it would be a world with MAD but without arms control.

MAD was of course a product of the cold war. It was a desperate makeshift in a desperate situation. Today, however, the cold war has long been over. The extreme peculiarity—or downright absurdity—of continuing to rely on MAD is that the political antagonism that underlay and justified it ended ten years ago, when the Soviet Union disappeared. During the cold war, the two powers threatened each other with annihilation for a reason; now they do so without a reason. Russia and the United States have no quarrel that would justify the firing of a single conventional round, not to speak of mutual annihilation. The human beings resolved their quarrels, but the weapons, displaying their characteristic astonishing immunity to political influence, evidently did not get the news. Here is a state of affairs that seems ripe for radical surgery.

NUCLEAR PROLIFERATION FUELED BY PEER PRESSURE

The second source of nuclear danger, proliferation, is most dramatically evident in South Asia, where India and Pakistan are engaged in the first nuclear face-off entirely unrelated to the cold war. It's difficult to predict where proliferation will occur next, but some of the main candidates are obvious: the Middle East, where Israel already possesses nuclear weapons and where Iraq and Iran are both known to be interested in acquiring them; and East Asia, where North Korea has well-developed nuclear and missile programs, and where Japan has . . . elected a prime minister who wishes to alter his nation's Constitution, which now forbids the development of offensive military forces, including nuclear weapons. If unchecked, proliferation has no logical or necessary stopping point. It points to a fully nuclearized world, in which any nation seriously threatened by another will feel itself fully entitled to build nuclear arms.

Unfortunately, the two basic elements of nuclear danger do not exist in separate worlds; they fatally interact in our one world. Most important, MAD is a standing invitation to proliferation, as the nuclearization of South Asia has already demonstrated. The simple, unavoidable truth is that possession fuels proliferation. If a country that feels threatened by the nuclear arms of another accepts MAD, as the nuclear powers teach them to do, they not only are likely to develop arms, they must do so. For a government to do otherwise would be to criminally abdicate its responsibility to defend its people. (Imagine the reactions in the United States, for example, if this country somehow did not possess nuclear arms but was suddenly threatened by a country that did possess them, and some third country lectured it on the virtues of remaining nuclear-weapon-free in the name of nonproliferation.)

Enter George W. Bush. His Administration has addressed the two major elements of nuclear danger in our world. In regard to the leftover cold war arsenals, he has proposed what on the face of it appears to be the most radical shift in policy since the inauguration of the MAD system. "The cold war logic that led to the creation of massive stockpiles on both sides," he has announced, in a refreshing acknowledgment of the new geopolitical reality, "is now outdated. Our mutual security need no longer depend on a nuclear balance of terror." The clear promise is of a fundamentally new policy, of a "new framework," in his words. In regard to proliferation, he has proposed to defend the United States with NMD (which was in fact embraced by President [Bill] Clinton and both parties in the Senate before Bush took office). In sum, "it is time to leave the cold war behind, and defend against the new threats of the twenty-first century." The Bush policies have the merit of acknowledging, in a way that the seemingly insensate continuation of MAD into the post–cold war world did not, the basic new realities—on the one hand, the collapse of MAD's political underpinnings and, on the other hand, the increasing dangers of proliferation. MAD acknowledges neither. It anachronistically deals with Russia exactly as we did during the cold war (though with somewhat reduced overkill), and it fatally undercuts nonproliferation by teaching that nuclear arsenals are the key to a nation's security. It is, indeed, the impossibility, in a MAD world, of framing effective nonproliferation policies that set the stage for NMD. If diplomacy wedded to MAD cannot stop proliferation, isn't it time to try something else, namely defenses? In that respect, NMD is the product of MAD.

The Bush prescription, however, does not work merely because the policies it purported to replace have failed. The most notable problem with the Bush approach is that it has not provided—even in theory—policies that can make its promises a reality. Bush seeks to offer an exit from the balance of terror, but he provides no actual escape route. MAD, notwithstanding its deficiencies, is a tough old bird, and cannot be waved away with a phrase in a speech. The closest Bush has come to a concrete policy in this field has been to announce a unilateral reduction in offensive nuclear arsenals to "the lowest possible number"— a number, however, that he has not specified. But a low number of offensive warheads, however welcome in itself (press reports have suggested that the range might be between 1,500 and 2,500 warheads), gives no release from the balance of terror. It preserves it at lower levels of overkill. (Picture the United States or Russia after a thousand or so of its cities have been destroyed.) In other passages of his speeches, Bush has seemed to acknowledge that MAD will stay in effect. In a speech on May 1 [2001], he stated in a less noted passage, "Deterrence can no longer be based solely on the threat of nuclear retaliation." The word "solely" is decisive. It means that MAD will be continued. At best, it will be supplemented by something, not replaced by it. What will that something be? Bush immediately continued, "Defenses can strengthen deterrence by reducing the incentive for proliferation." But to add defenses to MAD is a far different proposition from substituting one for the other.

That brings us to the second problem with the Bush plan. It is the one that has led almost the entire world to reject national missile defenses. Russia fears that a resurgent United States, feeling protected by its shield, will bully it in the future, and China fears that its small nuclear arsenal will be negated. The initial goal of NMD is to protect against proliferators. But at the same time, it would upset arms control. Defenses do not enhance the existing MAD system; they undermine it. That is why the world is upset that the Bush Administration wants to jettison the ABM treaty. Russian Foreign Minister Igor Ivanov, for example, has recently written, "With the ABM treaty as its root, a system of international accords on arms control and disarmament sprang up in the past decades. Inseparable from this process is the creation of global and regional regimes of nuclear nonproliferation. These agreements, comprising the modern architecture of international security, rest on the ABM treaty. If the foundation is destroyed, this interconnected system will collapse, nullifying thirty years of efforts by the world community." The United States' NATO allies have just made it clear that they agree.

In the nuclear sphere, defenses and offenses are oil and water. The addition of defenses destabilizes an offensive system and vice versa. MAD is an offensive framework, depending on mutual vulnerability to make everyone cautious. A defensive framework—a so-called defense-dominated world—is imaginable. Under it, offenses would be hugely reduced or eliminated by mutual agreement, and protection from residual danger would be provided by defenses. Only when defenses could clearly overwhelm any offense would a defensive system have been achieved. At that point, and only at that point, would MAD truly be a thing of the past. This was the vision put forward, at least rhetorically, by Ronald Reagan as his ultimate goal when he first proposed strategic defenses. Like MAD, defense domination qualifies as a true framework for nuclear danger. It is one that is in fact supported by many retired civilian and military officials, including the commander of the allied air forces in the Gulf War, Charles Horner, and Reagan's chief arms negotiator, Paul Nitze, both of whom have called for the elimination of nuclear weapons together with the creation of defenses. The only way, indeed, to make sense of antimissile defenses such as NMD is to wed them to a commitment by the nuclear powers to abolish nuclear weapons.

EVEN THE POSSIBILITY OF NMD UPSETS ARMS CONTROL

A further problem with NMD—certainly, the strangest one—is that so far it is a technical flop, having failed most of its tests.

Aristotle said that the most important attribute of a thing is existence. NMD lacks this attribute. Or, to put it differently, it has the attribute of nonexistence. It's been interesting to watch how this attribute has manifested itself politically. The Bush Administration announced that it means to "deploy" NMD. Deploy what, though? The Administration backed away from the Clinton plan—a limited deployment of ground-based missiles that would shoot down incoming missiles—and began to suggest even less-tested alternatives, including airborne, sea-based and space-based systems. When Bush recently sent his envoys to governments around the world to "persuade" them of the virtues of his plan, the governments learned to their surprise that nothing of a concrete character was on the table. It was one thing for Ivanov to say that "in order to hold a discussion, you have to have some subject for it, a plan, a concrete understanding of what the other side wants. For now, there are no such plans." It was another when the American envoy Paul Wolfowitz had to confess the truth of the charge, saying, "It is much too early, I think, even for us to ask people to agree with us, because we have not come to firm conclusions yet ourselves." The lesson may be that when you're promising pie in the sky, you should at least have some pie.

Is it possible that the nonexistence of NMD will spare us its harmful consequences? Unfortunately, not necessarily—unless the United States either abandons the scheme or weds it to a commitment to abolish nuclear weapons. Governments make their decisions according to future expectations. The looming possibility of NMD can therefore bring many of the disadvantages of actual deployment—disruption of arms control, pressure to proliferate—without any of the advantages. NMD thus creates a political problem that it cannot technically solve. When one reflects that the more ambitious NMD programs cannot be fully deployed (if they can work at all) until 2020, it becomes obvious that this is no minor consideration.

There is, we must note, one other "framework" that is possible: the framework of American military dominance, nuclear and otherwise, of the world. As the conservative commentators William Kristol and Robert Kagan have stated, Republicans "will ask Americans to face this increasingly dangerous world without illusions. They will argue that American dominance can be sustained for many decades to come, not by arms control agreements, but by augmenting America's power, and, therefore, its ability to lead." If the United States does abandon all nuclear arms control (perhaps, breaking out downward, in a manner of speaking, with unilateral cuts, the better to go upward again at will) in a bid for global dominance, and if it seeks to develop not only ballistic missile defense but—what may be more serious and technically feasible—offensive, space-based weapons, then our future framework will be neither MAD nor any version of defense dominance. It will be a hellbent military competition with the other powers of the earth—not just one but many arms races, and not, in all likelihood, in the nuclear sphere alone. Some countries will likely resort to the ugly little sisters of the family of mass destruction, chemical and biological weapons.

The great nuclear powers now rely on a system—MAD—that has lost political relevance to the world we live in. The Bush Administration has promised a new framework, in keeping with the needs of the time, but this collides both with itself and reality, political as well as technical. Absent a coherent global policy that actually does address the new shape of the nuclear predicament, events are likely to be driven in the vicious circle whose operations have already landed us in a world bristling with new nuclear dangers. Continued possession will fuel proliferation; proliferation will fuel hope for missile defense; missile defense (whether it can work or not) will disrupt arms control; and the disruption of arms control will, completing the circle, fuel proliferation. A second nuclear age has dawned, and it is running out of control. No new policies now on the horizon, in Washington or elsewhere, seem likely to turn things around anytime soon.

The Major Issues After September 11

DAVID KRIEGER

The attacks of September 11, 2001, continue to terrorize the United States, especially increasing public anxiety over the possibility of nuclear terrorism. David Krieger believes the U.S. government has done little to alleviate this fear.

What seems logical to Krieger—keeping nuclear weapons out of the hands of terrorists, achieving elimination of nuclear arsenals as well as nuclear testing for all time, and demonstrating to emerging nuclear powers that a nuclear arsenal is not necessary to national security, that a nuclear weapons–free world is possible—is currently but a dream. The United States has withdrawn from the 1972 Anti-Ballistic Missile Treaty, President George W. Bush has renewed his efforts to build and deploy a national missile defense system using space-based weapons to destroy incoming ballistic missiles (much like former President Ronald Reagan's "Star Wars" initiative), and the Pentagon is developing military contingency plans for the use of nuclear weapons against Russia, China, Iraq, Iran, North Korea, Libya, and Syria. If this course is not changed, Krieger warns, nuclear proliferation will be our undoing.

Krieger founded the Nuclear Age Peace Foundation and has served as its president since 1982. The foundation advocates peace through the abolition of nuclear weapons. Krieger is also a founding member of the Coordinating Committee of Abolition 2000, a global network of organizations committed to the worldwide elimination of nuclear weapons.

Shortly after the terrorist attacks of September 11, 2001, President [George W.] Bush gathered together his top security advisors to consider the implications of terrorism for US nuclear policy. A few facts were clear. There were well-organized and suicidal terrorists who were committed to inflicting large-scale damage on the US. These terrorists had attempted to obtain nuclear weapons and other weapons of mass destruction. They probably had not succeeded yet in obtaining nuclear weapons, but would certainly keep trying to do so. It was highly unlikely that terrorists would be able to deliver nuclear or other weapons of mass destruction by means of missiles, but they could potentially smuggle one or more nuclear weapons into the United States and use them to attack US cities. The death and destruction would be enormous, dwarfing the damage caused on September 11th.

A HOPEFUL NEW NUCLEAR WEAPONS POLICY

These facts alarmed the Bush security advisors. They went to work immediately developing plans to protect the American people against the possible nuclear terrorism that threatened American cities. The first prong of their defense against nuclear terrorism was to call for dramatically increased funding to secure the nuclear weapons in the former Soviet Union. Encouraged by the success that had been achieved up to this point with the Nunn–Lugar funding [an act introduced by Sam Nunn (D-GA) and Richard Lugar (R-IN) to provide funds for the storing or dismantling of weapons in the Soviet nuclear arsenal], they realized that this was an area in which they could work closely with Russia in assuring that these weapons were kept secure and out of the hands of criminals and terrorists. The Russians were eager to get this help and to join with the Americans in this effort to prevent nuclear terrorism.

The second prong of the US plan was to work with the Russians in achieving significant reductions in the nuclear arsenals of each country in order that there would be less nuclear weapons available to potentially fall into the hands of terrorists. Since the end of the Cold War the US and Russia have been reducing their nuclear arsenals, and now it was time to make even greater progress toward the promise of the two countries "to accomplish the total elimination of their nuclear arsenals." This meant reaching an agreement as a next step to slash the size of their arsenals to a few hundred nuclear warheads and to make these reductions irreversible. The international community applauded the boldness of this step, celebrating this major achievement in nuclear disarmament and this important step toward realizing the promise of the nuclear Non-Proliferation Treaty [originally adopted in 1968].

The third prong of the US plan was to give its full support to bringing the [1996] Comprehensive Test Ban Treaty into force, giving momentum to assuring an end to nuclear testing for all time. This step was viewed by the Bush security advisors as having indirect consequences for nuclear terrorism by assuring that other countries would forego the capability to improve the sophistication of their nuclear arsenals. It would be seen as a sign of US leadership for a world free of nuclear weapons, and this would have a positive effect on preventing further proliferation of nuclear weapons.

The fourth prong of the US plan was to reevaluate the administration's commitment to developing and deploying missile defenses. Prior to September 11th, President Bush and his security team had been strong advocates of developing and deploying ballistic missile defenses. President Bush had even been threatening to withdraw from the [1972] Anti-Ballistic Missile (ABM) Treaty in order to move forward with missile defense deployment. Following September 11th, it was clear that it made little sense to devote another $100 billion or more to missile defenses when terrorists were capable of attacking US cities by far simpler means. There were more urgent needs for these resources to be used in improving US intelligence and keeping nuclear weapons out of the hands of terrorists. Therefore, the decision was made to put the development of missile defenses on the back burner and instead devote major resources to safeguarding nuclear materials throughout the world. These actions were extremely helpful in improving our relations with both Russia and China, which were both relieved at not having to respond to our missile defenses by increasing their nuclear arsenals.

The fifth prong of the US plan was to work intensively with countries such as India, Pakistan and Israel to convince them that nuclear weapons were not in their security interests and that they would have a heavy price to pay if they did not join us in moving rapidly toward a nuclear-weapons-free world. The Bush advisors knew that this would be difficult, but they were certain that the US example of curtailing its own nuclear arsenal and foregoing missile defenses, along with support to these countries for economic development, would convince them to follow our lead.

A Harsh Reality: Disarmament and Non-Proliferation Are Only Dreams

The world's leaders and citizens have not heard about these US actions to combat nuclear terrorism because they never happened. The description above is an imaginative account of what might have happened—what should have happened. The most remarkable reality about the US response to the terrorist attacks of September 11, 2001, is how little these attacks actually affected US nuclear policy. Although US nuclear forces will certainly not deter terrorists, US nuclear policy remains highly dependent on nuclear weapons and the policy of nuclear deterrence.

To set the record straight, the Bush administration has supported cuts in the Nunn-Lugar funding for securing Russian nuclear weapons and materials. It has called for reductions in deployed strategic nuclear weapons over a ten-year period, although not within the scope of a binding treaty and, in fact, has indicated it plans to put the deactivated warheads on the shelf for potential future use. It has come out against ratification of the Comprehensive Test Ban Treaty, and boycotted a UN conference to bring the treaty into force more rapidly. President Bush has announced that the US will unilaterally withdraw from the Anti-Ballistic Missile Treaty, and move forward rapidly to deploy ballistic missile defenses, a move that has drawn critical response from both Russia and China. Finally, the Bush administration, rather than putting pressure on India and Pakistan to disarm, has ended the sanctions imposed on them for testing nuclear weapons in May 1998. The administration has never put pressure on Israel to eliminate its nuclear arsenal, although this is a major factor in motivating Arab countries to develop their own nuclear arsenals.

While there is much the Bush administration might have done to make nuclear terrorism less likely, the path they have chosen increases the risks of nuclear terrorism. It also undermines our relationship with countries we need in the fight against terrorism in general and nuclear terrorism in particular. Finally, the US nuclear policy after September 11th is a slap in the face to the 187 parties to the [1968] Non-Proliferation Treaty, and increases the possibilities of nuclear proliferation and a breakdown of the Non-Proliferation Treaty and regime.

CHAPTER 5

PERSONAL NARRATIVES AND VOICES OF PROTEST

AMERICAN
SOCIAL
MOVEMENTS

Putting a Human Face on the Cost of Nuclear War

KINUE TOMOYASU

Kinue Tomoyasu is a *hibakusha*—a Hiroshima survivor. Although the initial death toll from the U.S. atomic bombing of Hiroshima ranged between 130,000 and 150,000 by the end of 1945, the *hibakusha* now realize that the bomb's effects—radiation poisoning, birth defects, and cancer—threaten generation upon generation to come. In 1986 the Hiroshima Peace and Culture Foundation recorded the testimony of one hundred *hibakusha* to preserve the memory of this atrocity. Such testimony lends credibility to the antinuclear movement, putting a human face on the cost of nuclear war.

On August 6, 1945, forty-four-year-old Tomoyasu had just seen her daughter, Yatchan, off to the train station, but Tomoyasu returned home—just three miles from ground zero—because an air-raid warning had been issued. Yatchan, however, decided not to let the warning stop her from going to work. Following the initial blast, Tomoyasu was knocked unconscious by a blinding flash and breaking glass. When she came to, she went immediately into Hiroshima to search for Yatchan, but she did not find her daughter until the next day. Tomoyasu's only daughter died nine hours later, after suffering in unimaginable agony.

Before the bombing, Tomoyasu's husband had died from an illness. After the war, in which her son was forced to fight, her son committed suicide. Alone, Tomoyasu spent her remaining years in the Hiroshima Atomic Bomb Victims Nursing Home.

Excerpted from Kinue Tomoyasu's testimony to the Hiroshima Peace and Culture Foundation, September 29, 1999.

TOMOYASU: That morning [August 6, 1945] I left home with my daughter. She was working at the Industrial Research Institute. Then an air-raid warning was issued. I went back home, but my daughter insisted, "I'm going to the office," even though the air-raid warning had been issued. She reached the train station. The trains were always late in the morning, but they were on time that day. She took the train and when she got off at the station, she was hit by the A-bomb. I went inside my home since the warning was still on. I tucked myself in bed and waited for the warning to be lifted.

After the warning was lifted, I got up and folded the bedding, put it back into the closet, and opened the window. As I opened the window, there came the flash. It was so bright, a ten or hundred or thousand times brighter than a camera flash bulb. The flash was piercing my eyes and my mind went blank. The glass from the windows was shattered all over the floor. I was lying on the floor, too. When I came to, I was anxious to know what happened to my daughter, Yatchan. I looked outside the window and saw one of my neighbors. He was standing out there. I called, "Mr. Okamoto, what was that flash?" He said, "That was a killer beam." I became more anxious. I thought, "I must go, I must go and find her." I swept up the pieces of glass, put my shoes on, and took my air-raid hood with me. I made my way to a train station near Hiroshima. I saw a young girl coming my way. Her skin was dangling all over and she was naked. She was muttering, "Mother, water, mother, water." I took a look at her. I thought she might be my daughter, but she wasn't. I didn't give her any water. I am sorry that I didn't. But my mind was full, worrying about my daughter. I ran all the way to Hiroshima Station. Hiroshima Station was full of people. Some of them were dead, and many of them were lying on the ground, calling for their mothers and asking for water. I went to Tokiwa Bridge. I had to cross the bridge to get to my daughter's office. But there was a rope for tote across the bridge. And the people there told me, "You can't go beyond here today." I protested, "My daughter's office is over there. Please let me go through." They told me, "No."

Some men were daring to make the way through, but I couldn't go beyond it. I thought she might be on a way back home. I returned home, but my daughter was not back yet.

INTERVIEWER: Did you see the large cloud?

No, I didn't see the cloud.

You didn't see the mushroom cloud?

I didn't see the Mushroom cloud. I was trying to find my daughter. They told me I couldn't go beyond the bridge. I thought she might be back home, so I went back as far as Nikitsu Shrine. Then, the black rain started falling from the sky. And I wondered what it was. And it was what's called the black rain.

Can you tell us what was the black rain like?

It was like a heavy rain. And I had my air-raid hood on, so I didn't get it on my head fortunately, but it fell on my hands. And I ran and ran. I waited for her with the windows open. I stayed awake all night waiting and waiting for her, but she didn't come back. About six thirty on the morning of the 7th, Mr. Ishido, whose daughter was working at the same office with my daughter, came around. He called out asking for the To-moyasu's house. I went outside calling to him, "It's here, over here!" Mr. Ishido came up to me and said, "Quick! Get some clothes and go for her. Your daughter is at the bank of the Ota River." I said, "Thank you, thank you very much. Is she still alive?" He said, "She is alive," and added, "I'll show you the way." I took a yukata [kimono] with me. My neighbors offered me a stretcher. And I started running at full speed. People followed me and said, "Slow down! Be careful not to hurt yourself?" But still, I hurried as fast as I could. When I reached the Tokiwa Bridge, there were soldiers lying on the ground. Around Hiroshima Station, I saw more people lying dead, more on the morning of the 7th than on the 6th. When I reached the river bank, I couldn't tell who was who. I kept wondering where my daughter was. But then, she cried for me, "Mother!" I recognized her voice. I found her in a horrible condition. Her face looked terrible. And she still appears in my dreams like that sometimes. When I met her, she said, "There shouldn't be any war." The first thing she said to me was "Mother, it took you so long." I couldn't do anything for her. My neighbors went back home. They had wounded family members as well. I was all by myself, and I didn't know what to do. There were maggots in her wounds and a sticky yellowish pus, a white watery liquid coming out her wounds and a sticky yellowish liquid. I didn't know what was going on.

So you tried to remove the maggots from your daughter's body?

Yes. But her skin was just peeling right off. The maggots were coming out all over. I couldn't wipe them off. I thought it would be too painful. I picked off some maggots, though. She asked me what I was doing and I told her, "Oh, it's nothing." She nodded at my words. And nine hours later, she died.

You were holding her in your arms all that time?

Yes, on my lap. I had had bedding folded on the floor, but I held her in my arms. When I held her on my lap, she said, "I don't want to die." I told her, "Hang on. Hang on." She said, "I won't die before my brother comes home." But she was in pain and she kept crying, "Brother. Mother." On August 15th, I held her funeral. And around early October, my hair started to come out. I wondered what was happening to me, but all my hair was disappearing. In November, I became bald. Then, purple spots started to appear around my neck, my body and my arms, and on the inner parts of my thighs, a lot of them, all over, the purple spots all over my body. I had a high fever of forty degrees [Celsius (104°F)]. I was shivering and I couldn't consult the doctor. I still had a fever when I was admitted here [Hiroshima Atomic Bomb Victims Nursing Home] for a while, but now I don't have a fever so often.

After your son returned home from the war, what did he do?

He came back in February of 1946, and he took care of me. When he heard how his sister died, he said he felt so sorry for her. He told me he hated war. I understand. Many of his friends had died in the war. He told me he felt sorry that he survived. He was just filled with regret. My son got malaria during the war, also. He suffered a lot. I don't know why, but he became neurotic and killed himself, finally, by jumping in front of a train in October. I was left alone. I had to go through hardships, living alone. I have no family. I joined the White Chrysanthemum Organization at Hiroshima University, pledging to donate my body upon death for medical education and research. My registration number is number 1200. I'm ready. I'm ready now to be summoned by God at any moment. But God doesn't allow me to come to his side yet. If it were not for the war, my two children would not have died. If it were not for the war, I wouldn't have to stay at an institution like this. I suppose the three of us would have been living together in happiness. Ah, it is so hard on me.

Lamenting the Far-Reaching Destruction of the Atomic Bomb

DOROTHY DAY

The founder of the Catholic Worker Movement, Dorothy Day fought all of her life for a peace-loving, more spiritual world. The movement she founded continues to work toward solutions to world problems through Christian pacifism.

Day released the following statement on behalf of her movement in September 1945. In it she denounces the elation expressed by both President Harry Truman and the media over the "success" of the bombing. She calls the scientists murderers and mocks the account that they prayed during the initial testing of the bomb in the New Mexico desert. Day's lament is underscored by her dismay at people seeking the Catholic Church's opinion but failing to truly listen to its messages of love and peace.

Day died in 1980, but her supporters continue to protest war and violence of all forms.

Mr. Truman was jubilant. President Truman. True man; what a strange name, come to think of it. We refer to Jesus Christ as true God and true Man. Truman is a true man of his time in that he was jubilant. He was not a son of God, brother of Christ, brother of the Japanese, jubilating as he did. He went from table to table on the cruiser which was bringing him home from the Big Three conference, telling the great

Excerpted from "We Go on Record: The CW Response to Hiroshima," by Dorothy Day, *Catholic Worker*, www.catholicworker.org, September 1945. Copyright © 1945 by The Catholic Worker. Reprinted with permission.

news; "jubilant" the newspapers said. Jubilate Deo. We have killed 318,000 Japanese.

That is, we hope we have killed them, the Associated Press, on page one, column one of the *Herald Tribune,* says. The effect is hoped for, not known. It is to be hoped they are vaporized, our Japanese brothers—scattered, men, women and babies, to the four winds, over the seven seas. Perhaps we will breathe their dust into our nostrils, feel them in the fog of New York on our faces, feel them in the rain on the hills of Easton.

Jubilate Deo. President Truman was jubilant. We have created. We have created destruction. We have created a new element, called Pluto. Nature had nothing to do with it.

CREATED TO DESTROY

"A cavern below Columbia was the bomb's cradle," born not that men might live, but that men might be killed. Brought into being in a cavern, and then tried in a desert place, in the midst of tempest and lightning, tried out, and then again on the eve of the Feast of the Transfiguration of our Lord Jesus Christ, on a far off island in the eastern hemisphere, tried out again, this "new weapon which conceivably might wipe out mankind, and perhaps the planet itself."

"Dropped on a town, one bomb would be equivalent to a severe earthquake and would utterly destroy the place. A scientific brain trust has solved the problem of how to confine and release almost unlimited energy. It is impossible yet to measure its effects."

"We have spent two billion on the greatest scientific gamble in history and won," said President Truman jubilantly.

The papers list the scientists (the murderers) who are credited with perfecting this new weapon. One outstanding authority "who earlier had developed a powerful electrical bombardment machine called the cyclotron, was Professor O.E. Lawrence, a Nobel prize winner of the University of California. In the heat of the race to unlock the atom, he built the world's most powerful atom smashing gun, a machine whose electrical projectiles carried charges equivalent to 25,000,000 volts. But such machines were found in the end to be unnecessary. The atom of Uranium-235 was smashed with surprising ease. Science discovered that not sledgehammer blows, but subtle taps from slow traveling neutrons managed more on a tuning technique were all that were needed to disintegrate the Uranium-235 atom."

(Remember the tales we used to hear, that one note of a violin, if that note could be discovered, could collapse the Empire State Building. Remember too, that God's voice was heard not in the great and strong wind, not in the earthquake, not in the fire, but "in the whistling of a gentle air.")

MASS-PRODUCING DESTRUCTION

Scientists, army officers, great universities (Notre Dame included), and captains of industry—all are given credit lines in the press for their work of preparing the bomb—and other bombs, the President assures us, are in production now.

Great Britain controls the supply of uranium ore, in Canada and Rhodesia. We are making the bombs. This new great force will be used for good, the scientists assured us. And then they wiped out a city of 318,000. This was good. The President was jubilant.

Today's paper [September 1, 1945] with its columns of description of the new era, the atomic era, which this colossal slaughter of the innocents has ushered in, is filled with stories covering every conceivable phase of the new discovery. Pictures of the towns and the industrial plants where the parts are made are spread across the pages. In the forefront of the town of Oak Ridge, Tennessee is a chapel, a large comfortable-looking chapel benignly settled beside the plant. And the scientists making the first tests in the desert prayed, one newspaper account said.

THE CONSEQUENCES OF PLAYING GOD

Yes, God is still in the picture. God is not mocked. Today, the day of this so great news, God made a madman dance and talk, who had not spoken for twenty years. God sent a typhoon

Give Us Men to Match
Our Mountains

We need Men.

For seven dozen centuries
We have drifted onward,
Up over low strings of hills of progress,
Down across broad valleys of decadence.
History has been repeating itself.

But today that is all behind us.

The cracking of the atom
Broke the old historic vicious circle
Of bloody wars and uneasy truces
Among rival bands of
Little bigoted "patriots."

We now stand in the foothills

Of the lofty ranges of
The Atomic Age Mountains.
We can see their clear peaks
Rising above the misty foreground.

We cannot retreat.
We dare not hesitate.

We need Men.

We need Men of a new kind of valor,
A new measure of boldness.
We need dauntless men,
Men who have the inner strength
To break the chains
Of all old scattered loyalties,
All old outworn slogans.

We need Men,

Men who have the inner firmness
To clear their minds and
To disabuse their hearts
Of all old factional
Prepossessions.

We need Men

Who are willing
To Pause and look,
Men who are willing
To take the time to see
The Truth as it stands
Today unveiled.

We need men

Who are strong enough,
Modest enough, great enough,
Bold enough to join their hearts and minds
With other modest bold men
Of all the races
And nations of Human Kind
To invent a New United World.

We need men who will combine

Their strength with All Other Men
Into a Union of Universal Human Intelligence
And single-hearted Human Loyalty.

We need Men who will unite
In the great obvious task
Of creating a universal political union,
A United World
With One Unlimited Sovereignty.

Such Men can build
A World that will keep the peace,
A World that will march forward
And climb to the very summits of
The great mysterious peaks
Of the Atomic Age Mountains,

And on beyond them

To that pleasant country,
That New Promised Land
Of Triumphant Human Life.

MERRY CHRISTMAS, 1945
Edward Le Roy Moore, Director of World Peace Research

World Peace Research, Christmas mailing, 1945.

to damage the carrier *Hornet*. God permitted a fog to obscure vision and a bomber crashed into the Empire State Building. God permits these things. We have to remember it. We are held in God's hands, all of us, and President Truman too, and these scientists who have created death, but will use it for good. He, God, holds our life and our happiness, our sanity and our health; our lives are in His hands. *He is our Creator. Creator.*

And as I write, Pigsie, who works in Secaucus, New Jersey, feeding hogs, and cleaning out the excrement of the hogs, who comes in once a month to find beauty and surcease and glamour and glory in the drink of the Bowery, trying to drive the hell and the smell out of his nostrils and his life, sleeps on our doorstep, in this best and most advanced and progressive of all possible worlds. And as I write, our cat, Rainbow, slinks by with a shrill rat in her jaws, out of the kitchen closet here at Mott Street. Here in this greatest of cities which covered the cavern where this stupendous discovery was made, which institutes an era of unbelievable richness and power and glory for man. . . .

Everyone says, "I wonder what the Pope thinks of it?" How everyone turns to the Vatican for judgement, even though they do not seem to listen to the voice there! But our Lord Himself has already pronounced judgement on the atomic bomb. When James and John (John the beloved) wished to call down fire from heaven on their enemies, Jesus said:

"You know not of what spirit you are. The Son of Man came not to destroy souls but to save." He said also, "What you do unto the least of these my brethren, you do unto me."

Struggling Against the Nuclear Establishment

DOROTHY PURLEY

Uranium mining, begun in the 1930s, has devastated Dorothy Purley's village of Paguate on the Laguna Pueblo Reservation in New Mexico. Not only did the workers who mined the uranium develop cancer but also friends and family members through contaminated clothing and food. Only recently did the government, along with the mining operation, admit that they knew about the inherent danger in mining uranium but failed to ever warn Purley's tribe. After a long struggle against aggressive cancers and previously losing both her brother and mother to cancer, Purley passed away on December 2, 1999—fifty-seven years to the day that the first nuclear reactor was produced.

Purley spoke all over the world against the greed of the U.S. nuclear industry, and she became an inspiring nuclear abolitionist. Because she was too sick to travel in April 1999, the following speech—which details Purley's days in the mine and her subsequent battles against cancer, government, and big business, and the continual death and destruction of her people—was delivered by her daughter at the Global Hibakusha (Hiroshima survivors) delegation to the Hague Appeal for Peace conference.

My name is Dorothy Ann Purley. I have lived here in Paguate all my life. I worked at a time when the [uranium] mine was in process [in the 1970s] and not very long ago I found out I was diagnosed with cancer. Ever since, having to

Excerpted from "Uranium Mining and the Laguna People," by Dorothy Purley, www. greens.org, Spring 1996. Copyright © 1996 by Synthesis/Regeneration. Reprinted with permission.

go through chemotherapy, my health has really gone down, my immune system is not up to par any more. I just got back from a conference in Alaska; my Native American people there are dying out from cancer there too, as in the village of Paguate.

I've been working on health surveys. Wherever you go, people say it's because of the uranium mine; we were never told what precautions to take. . . . I worked there and I was never told how to be prepared to be in a safe way where . . . this cancer would have never come about. . . . It's up to God with whatever he gives you but I blame it on the mine because I worked eight years—everywhere—I worked as a security guard; as a safety office receptionist; at the hobo where they loaded the ore to transport it to the mill site in Grants [New Mexico]; at the crusher.

When the crusher got stuck we were down at the bottom using hammers to break the rocks down so the crusher could start going back up into processing, and I helped haul the ore from P9 where they were mining underground the richest ore that was coming out. We hauled back to the ore cars to have it transported. We came home, went to bed, never was a word that there was contamination of radiation. [I] just realized when I came to deal with this cancer, I found out. This cancer has really taught me a lot . . . and gotten me to a lot of places and I've realized what cancer really means.

SUFFERING THE CONSEQUENCES

When I first realized [I had cancer], I went [to have a free mammogram] and they realized I had two lumps on my right breast. . . . I was whisked away . . . and put on a machine. . . . The Doctor had spotted two tumors. A few days later I was called to say I was going to have . . . surgery done in Grants. I felt there was nothing wrong when I walked out [but] a few days later [the doctor informed me that I had lymphoma].

I had to get inputs from my son-in-law [to decide whether or not to have chemotherapy]. . . . My whole family went with me; this is where I really stood strongly, because my children, my father, my sister were all for me. My dad felt that it could have been him instead of me. He kept telling me, "Why is it you, my dear baby?. . . I don't have very much more to go, I should be leaving pretty soon.". . .

When I went for my first [chemotherapy treatment], it was like, "Am I going to see another tomorrow?" A lot of things went through my mind. . . . I usually had to stay in Albuquerque a day and a half, in case something went wrong. . . . They explained the medicine to me, it was a bunch of poison they were feeding me through my veins. . . . A week after the first chemotherapy, my hair started falling out. I was in the shower washing my hair and when I [saw] I had a whole handful, I started screaming and my daughter came running. . . . Within a month I became completely bald. . . . With the help of the prayers my people were sending me, I think that's what really kept me going. At times I feel like giving up, but . . . I have my grandchildren to think of.

LIVING PROOF

[The mine operated in Laguna Pueblo, where the village of Paguate is located] for 30 years. . . . I think I was the third woman that got hired. They used to blast sometimes four times a day. When there was no wind, that sulfur that they put in the blasting powder would just kind of sit over the village [just 1,000 feet away] and sometimes we had to cover our food. We . . . Indians dried our meat and some of our vegetables out in the sun; we never realized how much contamination there was in the air til we realized cancer was the main thing killing our people here in Paguate.

I miscarried three times; that's what really broke my heart. After that, I almost bled to death, I had to have surgery. There's quite a few that have had miscarriages and we have had deformed babies and 2 or 3 months ago there was a cat that had a litter that didn't have no tails at all. . . . We've had mentally retarded children here, and we have so much allergies. I have asthma too and bronchitis. Once when you come to find out what radiation can do . . . going to these conferences, you find out. But people are scared to ask, but some of these people that are so highly educated want to hide a lot of stuff, not letting us know.

We were asked to give a document. . . . I stood up at a village meeting and told them, "I'm living proof, I'm standing here, I have cancer, what more do you want?" We all know that our people are dying of cancer. In order to push something, you have to have a 100% backing from your community because only half a dozen [can't] do what has to be done. And that's why when I'm called to go somewhere, I go because I want people to know what's going on on the Laguna reservation.

COMPANIES MOTIVATED BY GREED

Any company that wants to come in, they better tell us what to expect, because other than that, it's just no more. We were told there is some company that wants to come back to re-open the mine. I said, "No way. Not over my dead body are they going to re-open. We've gone through enough." And what more do they want? We're losing our Laguna people, just like the Alaskan people. . . .

Right now, I'm glad the mine is closed, and the reclamation they did I don't appreciate. It makes me so sick just to ride through where once the mine was because I worked there and now I'm dealing with cancer. And I think it was very unfair for the companies hiding all the secrets and not being man or honest enough to say, "This is what you're going to expect. Are you going to accept or not?". . . The new generation . . . should be taught. . . . I feel my life is cheated on right now.

The reason nobody opened their mouth was because the bread and butter were placed on the table every weekend. Money is the maker of all evil. It's very sad what we're going through. People are crying out for help. One day, with God's will, that will straighten out. . . .

A PERSONAL CRUSADE

I've lost my mother, a brother who left four children. The youngest one didn't know who his father was. He keeps asking his older brothers, "How did it feel to have our dad around?" It's sad for a child to ask, how would it feel to have your dad to help you with problems, to hug you and to hold you, to tell you, "I love you very much." I still feel sad about it. [Her brother worked 30 years for Anaconda [the uranium mine], and she believes he died of undiagnosed stomach cancer, like their mother, who suffered severe stomach pain and wasted away before her death, which was attributed to heart failure. The nearest hospital was in Albuquerque.]

A lot of these things have to come to the surface, especially through the physicians that diagnose you with something that maybe they don't want you to know, but we do need to know. We need to be aware of what health hazards have accumulated on the reservation.

The ore was transported by [the] Santa Fe [railroad], to the mill site. No one has had the idea to sweep along the tracks to find out what kind of contamination [is there]—the crusher was on the east side of the village. The wind blows from the east, and we suffered a lot and the smell was really something terrible. . . . We had to go through all this hell; to me it was like during the Vietnam war, how this blasting—you could actually hear the rocks fall back to the surface. There was a lot of cracks [in the houses], the homes have been jarred so much, they're hard to put back together. . . . We were told it didn't have to do with the mine blasting, but some of us Native Americans aren't dumb! We know what technology is, now . . . it's just a shame how we Indians are crying out for help, yet DOE [Department of Energy] doesn't understand. I think we need to push.

Anyway, I sit here, day after day in Paguate, still suffering. I'm proud to be a Native American Indian from Laguna, who was diagnosed with cancer, whose life has been shortened. But I'm going to keep struggling for better tomorrows, [and] I hope to continue to do what I have to, to be happy and say what I have to.

How Do We Avoid a Nuclear Holocaust?

JONATHAN SCHELL

Writer, journalist, and professor Jonathan Schell has become a leading advocate of nuclear abolition within the contemporary antinuclear movement. This current role began with his publication *The
Fate of the Earth*, in which Schell explores the horrific effects of a
nuclear holocaust. In the following selection he concludes that only
a political solution can ensure the survival of humanity.

   Schell argues that if nations can learn to resolve disputes through
peaceful means, then disarmament—of both nuclear *and* conventional weapons—would logically follow. Although he acknowledges
that an initial weapons freeze would move this radical change forward, Schell sees nothing less than total disarmament as the key to
Earth's survival. If we do not learn tolerance and nonviolence—and
learn them at once—then Schell believes that we will be signing our
planet's death warrant.

I n supposing for a moment that the world had found a political means of making international decisions, I made a
very large supposition indeed—one that encompasses something close to the whole work of resolving the nuclear
predicament, for, once a political solution has been found, disarmament becomes a merely technical matter, which should
present no special difficulties. And yet simply to recognize that
the task is at bottom political, and that only a political solution
can prepare the way for full disarmament and real safety for the
species, is in itself important. The recognition calls attention
to the fact that disarmament in isolation from political change
cannot proceed very far. It alerts us to the fact that when

someone proposes, as President [Jimmy] Carter did in his Inaugural Address, to aim at ridding the world of nuclear weapons, there is an immense obstacle that has to be faced and surmounted. For the world, in freeing itself of one burden, the peril of extinction, must inevitably shoulder another: it must assume full responsibility for settling human differences peacefully. Moreover, this recognition forces us to acknowledge that nuclear disarmament cannot occur if conventional arms are left in place, since as long as nations defend themselves with arms of any kind they will be fully sovereign, and as long as they are fully sovereign they will be at liberty to build nuclear weapons if they so choose. And if we assume that wars do break out and some nations find themselves facing defeat in the conventional arena, then the reappearance of nuclear arms, which would prevent such defeat, becomes a strong likelihood. What nation, once having entrusted its fortunes to the force of arms, would permit itself to be conquered by an enemy when the means of driving him back, perhaps with a mere threat, was on hand? And how safe can the world be while nations threaten one another's existence with violence and retain for themselves the sovereign right to build whatever weapons they choose to build? This vision of an international life that in the military sphere is restricted to the pre-nuclear world while in the scientific realm it is in the nuclear world is, in fact, thoroughly implausible. If we are serious about nuclear disarmament—the minimum technical requirement for real safety from extinction—then we must accept conventional disarmament as well, and this means disarmament not just of nuclear powers but of all powers, for the present nuclear powers are hardly likely to throw away their conventional arms while non-nuclear powers hold on to theirs. But if we accept both nuclear and conventional disarmament, then we are speaking of revolutionizing the politics of the earth. The goals of the political revolution are defined by those of the nuclear revolution. We must lay down our arms, relinquish sovereignty, and found a political system for the peaceful settlement of international disputes.

The task we face is to find a means of political action that will permit human beings to pursue any end for the rest of time. We are asked to replace the mechanism by which political decisions, whatever they may be, are reached. In sum, the task is nothing less than to reinvent politics: to reinvent the world. However, extinction will not wait for us to reinvent the world. Evolution was slow to produce us, but our extinction will be swift; it will literally be over before we know it. We have to match swiftness with swiftness. Because everything we do and everything we are is in jeopardy, and because the peril is immediate and unremitting, every person is the right person to act and every moment is the right moment to begin, starting with the present moment. For nothing underscores our common humanity as strongly as the peril of extinction does; in fact, on a practical and political plane it establishes that common humanity. The purpose of action, though, is not to replace life with politics. The point is not to turn life into a scene of protest; life is the point.

VOICING THE REQUIREMENTS OF SURVIVAL

Whatever the eventual shape of a world that has been reinvented for the sake of survival, the first, urgent, immediate step, which requires no deep thought or long reflection, is for each person to make known, visibly and unmistakably, his desire that the species survive. Extinction, being in its nature outside human experience, is invisible, but we, by rebelling against it, can indirectly make it visible. No one will ever witness extinction, so we must bear witness to it before the fact. And the place for the rebellion to start is in our daily lives. We can each perform a turnabout right where we are—let our daily business drop from our hands for a while, so that we can turn our attention to securing the foundation of all life, out of which our daily business grows and in which it finds its justification. This disruption of our lives will be a preventive disruption, for we will be hoping through the temporary suspension of our daily life to ward off the eternal suspension of it in extinction. And this turnabout in the first instance can be as simple as a phone call to a friend, a meeting in the community.

However, even as the first steps are taken, the broad ultimate requirements of survival must be recognized and stated clearly. If they are not, we might sink into self-deception, imagining that inadequate measures would suffice to save us. I would suggest that the ultimate requirements are in essence the two that I have mentioned: global disarmament, both nuclear and conventional, and the invention of political means by which the world can peacefully settle the issues that throughout history it has settled by war. Thus, the first steps and the ultimate requirements are clear. If a busload of people is speeding down a mountainside toward a cliff, the passengers do not convene a seminar to investigate the nature of their predicament; they see to it that the driver applies the brakes. Therefore, at a minimum, a freeze on the further deployment of nuclear weapons, participated in both by countries that now have them and by countries that do not yet have them, is called for. Even better would be a reduction in nuclear arms—for example, by cutting the arsenals of the superpowers in half, as George Kennan suggested [during the early 1980s]. Simultaneously with disarmament, political steps of many kinds could be taken. For example, talks could be started among the nuclear powers with the aim of making sure that the world did not simply blunder into extinction by mistake; technical and political arrangements could be drawn up to reduce the likelihood of mechanical mistakes and misjudgments of the other side's intentions or actions in a time of crisis, and these would somewhat increase the world's security while the predicament was being tackled at a more fundamental level. For both superpowers—and, indeed, for all other powers—avoiding extinction is a common interest than which none can be greater. And since the existence of a common interest is the best foundation for negotiation, negotiations should have some chance of success. However, the existence of negotiations to reduce the nuclear peril would provide no reason for abandoning the pursuit of other things that one believed in, even those which might be at variance with the beliefs of one's negotiating partner. Thus, to give one contemporary example, there is no need, or excuse, for the United States not to take strong measures to oppose Soviet-sponsored repression in Poland just because it is engaged in disarmament talks with the Soviet Union. The world will not end if we suspend shipments of wheat to the Soviet Union. On the other hand, to break off those talks in an effort to help the Poles, who will be as extinct as anyone else if a holocaust comes about, would be self-defeating. To seek to "punish" the other side by breaking off those negotiations would be in reality self-punishment. All the limited aims of negotiation can be pursued in the short term without danger if only the ultimate goal is kept unswervingly in mind. But ordinary citizens must insist that all these things be done, or they will not be.

TOLERANCE, NONVIOLENCE, AND LIBERTY

If action should be concerted, as it eventually must be, in a common political endeavor, reaching across national boundaries, then, just as the aim of the endeavor would be to hold the gates of life open to the future generations, so its method would be to hold its own gates open to every living person. But it should be borne in mind that even if every person in the world were to enlist, the endeavor would include only an infinitesimal fraction of the people of the dead and the unborn generations, and so it would need to act with the circumspection and modesty of a small minority. From its mission to preserve all generations, it would not seek to derive any rights to dictate to the generations on hand. It would not bend or break the rules of conduct essential to a decent political life, for it would recognize that once one started breaking rules in the name of survival no rule would go unbroken. Intellectually and philosophically, it would carry the principle of tolerance to the utmost extreme. It would attempt to be as open to new thoughts and feelings as it would be to the new generations that would think those thoughts and feel those feelings. Its underlying supposition about creeds and ideologies would be that whereas without mankind none can exist, with mankind all can exist. For while the events that might trigger a holocaust would probably be political, the consequences would be deeper than any politics or political aims, bringing ruin to the hopes and plans of capitalists and socialists, rightists and leftists, conservatives and liberals alike. Having as the source of its strength only the spontaneously offered support of the people of the earth, it would, in turn, respect each person's will, which is to say his liberty. Eventually, the popular will that it marshalled might be deployed as a check on the power of whatever political institutions were invented to replace war.

Since the goal would be a nonviolent world, the actions of this endeavor would be nonviolent. What Gandhi once said of the spirit of nonviolent action in general would be especially important to the spirit of these particular actions: "In the dictionary of nonviolent action, there is no such thing as an 'external enemy.'" With the world itself at stake, all differences would by definition be "internal" differences, to be resolved on the basis of respect for those with whom one disagreed. If our aim is to save humanity, we must respect the humanity of every person. For who would be the enemy? Certainly not the world's political leaders, who, though they now menace the earth with nuclear weapons, do so only with our permission, and even at our bidding. At least, this is true for the democracies. We do not know what the peoples of the totalitarian states, including the people of the Soviet Union, may want. They are locked in silence by their government. In these circumstances, public opinion in the free countries would have to represent public opinion in all countries, and would have to bring its pressure to bear, as best it could, on all governments.

WE MUST CHOOSE—LIFE OR DEATH?

At present, most of us do nothing. We look away. We remain calm. We are silent. We take refuge in the hope that the holocaust won't happen, and turn back to our individual concerns. We deny the truth that is all around us. Indifferent to the future of our kind, we grow indifferent to one another. We drift apart. We grow cold. We drowse our way toward the end of the world. But if once we shook off our lethargy and fatigue and began to act, the climate would change. Just as inertia produces despair—a despair often so deep that it does not even know itself as despair—arousal and action would give us access to hope, and life would start to mend: not just life in its entirety but daily life, every individual life. At that point, we would begin to withdraw from our role as both the victims and the perpetrators of mass murder. We would no longer be the destroyers of mankind but, rather, the gateway through which the future generations would enter the world. Then the passion and will that we need to save ourselves would flood into our lives. Then the walls of indifference, inertia, and coldness that now isolate each of us from others, and all of us from the past and future generations, would melt, like snow in spring. [Writer] E.M. Forster told us, "Only connect!" Let us connect. [Poet W.H.] Auden told us, "We must love one another or die." Let us love one another—in the present and across the divides of death and birth. Christ said, "I come not to judge the world but to save the world." Let us, also, not judge the world but save the world. By restoring our severed links with life, we will restore our own lives. Instead of stopping the course of time and cutting off the human future, we would make it possible for the future generations to be born. Their inestimable gift to us, passed back from the future into the present, would be the wholeness and meaning of life.

Two paths lie before us. One leads to death, the other to life. If we choose the first path—if we numbly refuse to acknowledge the nearness of extinction, all the while increasing our preparations to bring it about—then we in effect become the allies of death, and in everything we do our attachment to life will weaken: our vision, blinded to the abyss that has opened at our feet, will dim and grow confused; our will, discouraged by the thought of trying to build on such a precarious foundation anything that is meant to last, will slacken; and we will sink into stupefaction, as though we were gradually weaning ourselves from life in preparation for the end. On the other hand, if we reject our doom, and bend our efforts toward survival—if we arouse ourselves to the peril and act to forestall it, making ourselves the allies of life—then the anesthetic fog will lift: our vision, no longer straining not to see the obvious, will sharpen; our will, finding secure ground to build on, will be restored; and we will take full and clear possession of life again. One day—and it is hard to believe that it will not be soon—we will make our choice. Either we will sink into the final coma and end it all or, as I trust and believe, we will awaken to the truth of our peril, a truth as great as life itself, and, like a person who has swallowed a lethal poison but shakes off his stupor at the last moment and vomits the poison up, we will break through the layers of our denials, put aside our fainthearted excuses, and rise up to cleanse the earth of nuclear weapons.

Estimated Nuclear Weapons Stockpiles, 1990–2003

Nuclear Warheads

Delivery Vehicles	1990		January 1997						2003 (projected)	
	United States	Soviet Union	United States	Russian Federation	China	France	United Kingdom	Global Total	United States	Russian Federation
ICBM Warheads	2,450	6,612	2,075	3,577	17	0	0	5,670	500	605
SLBM Warheads	5,760	2,804	3,264	2,272	12	384	140	6,070	1,680	1,696
Bomber Weapons	4,508	1,363	1,800	820	120	0	0	2,740	1,320	810
Total Strategic Warheads	**12,720**	**10,780**	**7,150**	**6,670**	**149**	**384**	**140**	**14,500**	**3,500**	**3,100**
Non-Strategic Nuclear Warheads	7,147	11,350	1,150	4,400	246	65	100	5,960	950	2,750
Reserve/Inactive Nuclear Weapons	3,423	15,879	7,100	8,000–10,000	n.a.	n.a.	n.a.	15,100–17,100	5,000	5,000
Total Nuclear Weapons Stockpile	**23,000**	**38,000**	**15,400**	**20,000–22,000**	**400**	**450**	**240**	**36,000–38,000**	**10,000**	**10,850**

Nuclear Delivery Vehicles

Delivery Vehicles	1990		January 1997						2003 (projected)	
	United States	Soviet Union	United States	Russian Federation	China	France	United Kingdom	Global Total	United States	Russian Federation
ICBM	1,000	1,398	575	738	7/10	n.a.	n.a.	1,330	500	605
SLBM/SSBN	672	940	408/17	440/26	12/1	64/4	28/2	952	336	408
Heavy Bombers/ Weapons	280	162	(179)/102	79	120	n.a.	n.a.	301	87	69
Non-Strategic	—	—	—	—	126	69	96	291	—	—
Total Delivery Vehicles	**1,952**	**2,500**	**1,085**	**1,257**	**275**	**133**	**124**	**2,874**	**923**	**1,082**

Compiled by Melinda Lamont-Havers, the Coalition to Reduce Nuclear Dangers, danger@stimson.org. Figures based on the latest available information from the Natural Resources Defense Council, Arms Control Association, the International Institute for Strategic Studies and government sources. Numbers may not add due to rounding.

GLOSSARY

antiballistic missile (ABM): An ABM is a missile that is used to intercept ballistic missiles. Since the 1960s, both the United States and Russia have attempted to develop ABM systems to counter ballistic missiles, which are launched into space by a booster rocket and then descend toward a target in a free fall. In 1972, both nations signed the ABM Treaty, allowing each nation to possess only two ABM deployment sites. President Ronald Reagan's failed Strategic Defense Initiative (see *SDI*) and President George W. Bush's current National Missile Defense (see *NMD*) program are both ABM systems.

Atomic Energy Commission (AEC): The AEC was a civilian agency of the U.S. government established by the Atomic Energy Act of 1946. Its main goal was to administer and regulate the production and use of atomic power. Under the Energy Reorganization Act of October 1974, the AEC was abolished and two new federal agencies were established in its place: the Energy Research and Development Administration, which was absorbed by the Department of Energy in 1977, and the Nuclear Regulatory Commission (see *NRC*).

Comprehensive Test Ban Treaty (CTBT): The CTBT was signed by President Bill Clinton on September 24, 1996. To take effect, this international treaty, which bans all nuclear weapons test explosions, must be ratified by all forty-four nations that were members of the Conference on Disarmament as of June 18, 1996. As of March 2002, however, India and Pakistan had not signed the treaty, and China, Russia, and the United States had not ratified it.

Cooperative Threat Reduction (CTR) program: The CTR program was introduced in 1991 by Senators Sam Nunn

(D–Ga.) and Richard Lugar (R–Ind.). The CTR program allows the U.S. Department of Defense to assist former Soviet states in dismantling and destroying nuclear weapons, strengthening the security of nuclear weapons sites, and preventing proliferation.

intercontinental ballistic missile (ICBM): An ICBM is a land-based missile with a range of thirty-four hundred miles or more.

Intermediate–Range Nuclear Forces (INF) Treaty: This treaty, signed by the United States and the Soviet Union in 1987, banned all land-based missiles with ranges between three hundred and thirty-four hundred miles. This was the first time an entire class of nuclear weapons was banned.

multiple independently targetable reentry vehicles (MIRVs): These vehicles were first deployed by the United States in 1970 on the Minuteman III missile, an intercontinental ballistic missile (see *ICBM*) that is still part of the U.S. nuclear arsenal today.

mutual assured destruction (MAD): MAD became official military doctrine in the early 1960s, patterned after President Dwight D. Eisenhower's New Look policy, which held that U.S. nuclear capability was the major Soviet deterrent—psychologically as well as politically. According to MAD, once the United States and the Soviet Union each had a large enough nuclear arsenal, a first strike by either side would be highly unlikely.

National Committee for a Sane Nuclear Policy (SANE): SANE was established in the late 1950s by a group of writers, editors, and peace activists—including Albert Schweitzer, Eleanor Roosevelt, Bertrand Russell, and Martin Luther King Jr.—who were willing to protest U.S. nuclear policy. SANE became a significant voice in the antinuclear debate, contributing to the ratification of the Limited Nuclear Test Ban Treaty in 1963 and the Treaty on the Nonproliferation of Nuclear Weapons in 1968.

National Missile Defense (NMD) program: The NMD program, a resurrected form of President Ronald Reagan's Strategic Defense Initiative (see *SDI*), was shot down in 2000 by President Bill Clinton but picked up in 2001 by President George W. Bush. Antinuclear activists believed that this program would threaten the Antiballistic Missile Treaty (see *ABM*) of 1972 and create a new arms race between the United States and Russia. In December 2001, President Bush brought this fear closer to reality by officially withdrawing the United States from the ABM Treaty and riling Russian president Vladimir Putin.

Nevada test site (NTS): Formerly named the Nevada proving grounds in 1951 by President Harry S. Truman, the NTS is the location of atmospheric testing of nuclear bombs.

North American Aerospace Defense Command (NORAD): NORAD formerly the North American Air Defense Command, was established in 1958 as an agreement between Canada and the United States for a joint command of continental air defense. It underwent its name change in 1985 to reflect the growing threat of intercontinental ballistic missiles (see *ICBM*).

North Atlantic Treaty Organization (NATO): NATO was established on April 4, 1949, by twelve nations: Belgium, Canada, Denmark, France, Iceland, Italy, Luxembourg, the Netherlands, Norway, Portugal, the United Kingdom, and the United States. Although the original intent of the treaty was to deter Soviet aggression in Europe, NATO continues to face fresh challenges to peace in the West, for which it has retained its military capability, and continues to work toward its original goal of uniting Europe with North America, though its expansion goal may soon include Baltic states as well. In October 2001, Russian president Vladimir Putin became the first Russian leader to visit NATO headquarters. In return for this gesture, Russia was given a voice, though not voting power, in NATO affairs.

Nuclear Regulatory Commission (NRC): The NRC is an independent U.S. government agency that was established in 1975 under the 1974 Energy Reorganization Act to replace the Atomic Energy Commission (see *AEC*). The NRC's focus is the use of nuclear energy to generate electric power. To that end, the NRC licenses the construction and operation of nuclear reactors and other nuclear facilities as well as the possession, use, processing, transport, handling, and disposal of nuclear materials.

Strategic Arms Limitation Talks (SALT): These talks took place between the United States and Soviet Union from 1969 to 1979. This forum allowed each side to develop a better understanding of the other's policies and beliefs, which in turn facilitated their discussions of arms reductions.

Strategic Arms Reduction Treaty (START): START was signed by the United States and Russia in 1991. It required the elimination of almost 50 percent of the nuclear warheads carried by ballistic missiles.

Strategic Defense Initiative (SDI): SDI was a program initiated by President Ronald Reagan in 1983 to research and develop a space based–defense system that would use lasers to shoot down incoming Soviet missiles. SDI never proved feasible, and the media facetiously dubbed it the "Star Wars" project.

Theater Missile Defense (TMD): TMD, a type of anti-ballistic missile (see *ABM*) system, is a defensive system placed on ships, on land, and in the air for regional protection against ballistic missile attack.

Threshold Test Ban Treaty (TTBT): The TTBT was signed by the United States and Soviet Union in 1974 to limit nuclear test explosions to under 150 kilotons (which is nearly ten times greater than the explosion created by the bomb dropped on Hiroshima).

Treaty on the Nonproliferation of Nuclear Weapons (NPT): The NPT was signed in Washington, London, and Moscow on July 1, 1968. It required the signers to "pursue negotiations in good faith on effective measures relating to cessation of the nuclear arms race at an early date and to nuclear disarmament" to take place under international control.

Underground Nuclear Explosions for Peaceful Purposes (PNE) Treaty: This treaty was signed by the United States and Soviet Union in 1976. It limited single explosions to 150 kilotons (which is more than ten times greater than the explosion created by the bomb dropped on Hiroshima) and multiple explosions to 1,500 kilotons. Even though the treaty was never ratified, both nations nonetheless honored its terms.

Union of Soviet Socialist Republics (USSR): The USSR, commonly known as the Soviet Union, was an organization of states from the former Russian Empire in Eastern Europe and Asia. Moscow was its capital. Under Communist dictatorship, the Soviet Union was the West's chief rival following World War II and a leading force in international affairs until its collapse in 1991.

Chronology

1934
Enrico Fermi achieves the world's first nuclear fission.

1939
January 29: Scientist Robert Oppenheimer realizes the possibility of an atomic bomb.
August 2: Einstein writes to President Franklin D. Roosevelt (FDR), urging development of an atomic bomb before the Nazis develop one.

1941
December 6: FDR authorizes the Manhattan Project to develop an atomic bomb.

1945
May 31: FDR decides to drop an atomic bomb on Japan.
August 6: The United States drops an atomic bomb, dubbed Little Boy, on Hiroshima, Japan. It has a yield equivalent to fifteen kilotons of TNT.
August 9: The United States drops a second atomic bomb, dubbed Fat Man, on Nagasaki, Japan.
August 14: Japan surrenders.
September 20: The United States adopts a first-strike nuclear warfare policy.
December: Manhattan Project scientist Eugene Rabinowitch spearheads the creation of the Atomic Scientists of Chicago and the first issue of the publication *The Bulletin of the Atomic Scientist*.

1946
July 1: The United States begins nuclear weapons testing at the Bikini Atoll in the Pacific Ocean.
August 1: Under the Atomic Energy Act, the U.S. Congress establishes its own Atomic Energy Commission (AEC) to control U.S. nuclear energy development.

November 10: Soviet scientists assemble the first full-scale nuclear reactor.

1948

April: The U.S. AEC continues nuclear weapons testing at Eniwetok Atoll in the Pacific Ocean.

1949

April 4: The North Atlantic Treaty Organization (NATO) is established to unite U.S. and European countries against the perceived Soviet aggression.

August 29: The Soviet Union detonates its first atomic bomb, Joe 1 (ten to twenty kilotons), in Kazakhstan.

December 2: In a classified experiment the Hanford Nuclear Plant in Washington State releases three tons of irradiated uranium fuel to duplicate the pollution output from a Soviet reactor.

1950

November 30: President Truman confirms that the United States is considering the use of nuclear weapons in Korea.

December: The first production of electricity from atomic fission occurs at the National Reactor Testing Station in Idaho.

1951

January 11: President Truman approves the establishment of the Nevada Proving Grounds, later called the Nevada Test Site (NTS), where atmospheric tests of U.S. nuclear weapons will take place.

1952

November 1: The United States detonates the first hydrogen bomb, 10.4 megaton Mike, at Eniwetak Atoll in the Pacific Ocean.

1954

January 21: The USS *Nautilus* (SSN 571), the world's first nuclear-powered submarine, is launched by the navy.

March 1: Bravo, a seventeen megaton hydrogen bomb detonated by the United States at the Bikini Atoll in the Pacific

Ocean, contaminates a Japanese fishing boat, *Lucky Dragon*, and residents of Rongelap and Utirik.

1956
July–August: The first nuclear power plant begins production at Obinsk in the Soviet Union and Calder Hall in England.

1957
July 2: The first Pugwash Conference is held in Pugwash, Nova Scotia. Twenty-two scientists from ten countries attend.
July 29: The UN establishes the International Atomic Energy Agency to promote peaceful uses of nuclear energy.
August 6: The first organized U.S. demonstration against nuclear weapons testing takes place at the Nevada Test Site and results in the arrest of eleven protesters.
November 15: The National Committee for a Sane Nuclear Policy (SANE) is founded.

1958
January 15: Scientist Linus Pauling issues a petition to stop the testing of nuclear bombs. The petition is signed by 11,021 scientists.
March 11: A U.S. bomber accidentally drops a nuclear bomb over Mars Bluff, South Carolina. It leaves a crater seventy-five feet wide and thirty-five feet deep.
October 31: President Eisenhower declares a moratorium on all nuclear weapons testing.

1959
October 31: The United States deploys the first intercontinental ballistic missile (ICBM), the *Atlas D*.

1960
October 5: A radar malfunction leads the North American Aerospace Defense Command (NORAD) to believe a massive missile attack has been launched against North America.

1961
September 15: The U.S. moratorium on nuclear weapons testing ends.

September 20: The United States and Soviet Union enter disarmament negotiations.

1962

The United States now has two hundred nuclear power reactors in operation.

October 16–29: The Cuban Missile Crisis threatens to escalate into a full-scale nuclear war between the United States and the Soviet Union.

1963

April 11: Pope John XXIII calls for an end to the nuclear arms race.

June 10: President John F. Kennedy declares a moratorium on atmospheric testing of nuclear weapons.

August 5: The Partial Test Ban Treaty is signed by the United States and the Soviet Union.

1968

July 1: The Treaty on Non-Proliferation of Nuclear Weapons (NPT) is signed in Washington, Moscow, and London.

1969

November 17: The first Strategic Arms Limitation Talks (SALT) between the United States and the Soviet Union begin in Helsinki, Finland.

1970

April 16: The main series of SALT begins in Vienna.

August 19: The United States deploys the first missile with multiple independently targetable reentry vehicles (MIRVs), the *Minuteman III*.

December 18: Scientists deliberately release a radioactive cloud from a ten-kiloton underground explosion in Nevada in order to test the environmental effects of the cloud. It floats all the way to Canada.

1972

May 26: SALT I ends with President Richard M. Nixon and Soviet general secretary Leonid Brezhnev signing the Anti-Ballistic Missile (ABM) Treaty.

1974

July 3: The Threshold Test Ban Treaty (TTBT) is signed by the United States and Soviet Union to limit test nuclear weapons to under 150 kilotons.

November 23: The Vladivostok Accord is signed by the United States and the Soviet Union to initiate SALT II.

1976

May 28: The Underground Nuclear Explosions for Peaceful Purposes (PNE) Treaty is signed by the United States and Soviet Union to limit single explosions to 150 kilotons and multiple explosions to fifteen hundred kilotons.

1977

July 7: The United States tests a neutron bomb, a small hydrogen bomb with only one-tenth of the blast, heat, and fallout produced by a full-size hydrogen bomb. It is designed to disable troops by producing a shower of neutrons that can pass through steel and concrete.

1979

March 28: The Three Mile Island nuclear power plant leaks radiation into the surrounding areas of central Pennsylvania, including Harrisburg, the state capital.

March 31: Dr. Helen Caldicott, an Australian pediatrician and antinuclear activist, revives Physicians for Social Responsibility, which previously had exposed the effects of fallout radiation from nuclear weapons testing on human breast milk and children's teeth.

June 18: The SALT II treaty is signed by the United States and Soviet Union in Vienna, Austria, which establishes a cap of twenty-four hundred strategic offensive weapons.

November 9: For six minutes, a nuclear missile attack simulation is misinterpreted as a real attack. U.S. fighter planes take off from U.S. and Canadian bases, and U.S. nuclear weapons installations around the globe are placed on alert before the mistake is discovered.

December: NATO places nuclear missiles in Europe while simultaneously negotiating for their removal.

December 27: President Jimmy Carter rejects the SALT II Treaty after the Soviet Union invades Afghanistan.

1982

March 10: Democratic senator Edward M. Kennedy and Republican senator Mark O. Hatfield introduce a U.S. Senate resolution calling for a freeze on the testing, production, and further deployment of nuclear warheads, missiles, and other delivery systems within the United States and Soviet Union.

June 12: One million people gather in New York City's Central Park to support the second UN Special Session on Disarmament. It is the largest antiwar demonstration in history.

July 20: President Ronald Reagan removes the United States from ongoing talks regarding the Comprehensive Test Ban Treaty (CTBT).

December 28: The Nuclear Age Peace Foundation is founded.

1983

March 23: President Reagan introduces the Strategic Defense Initiative (SDI) program to research and develop a space-based defense system.

1984

October 10: Based on reports that the Soviet Union has violated several arms control treaties, President Reagan continues the U.S. rejection of the SALT II Treaty.

1986

January 15: Soviet president Mikhail Gorbachev calls for the abolition of all nuclear weapons by 2000.

April 26: Reactor No. 4 of the Chernobyl nuclear power plant in the Ukraine explodes and sends a radioactive cloud around the world. It releases around 50 million curies of radiation.

October 11–12: Presidents Reagan and Gorbachev meet in Iceland to discuss the possibility of nuclear abolition. The talks end when President Reagan refuses to abandon his SDI program.

December 11: The South Pacific Nuclear-Free-Zone Treaty enters into force.

1987

February 26: The Soviet Union ends an eighteen-month moratorium on nuclear testing, which they offer to resume only if the United States will enact a similar moratorium.

December 8: The Intermediate-Range Nuclear Forces (INF) Treaty is signed by the United States and Soviet Union.

1990

June 1: Presidents George H.W. Bush and Gorbachev sign new protocols to the TTBT and PNE Treaty to provide for advance notification and onsite inspection of tests involving weapons above thirty-five kilotons.

November 16: The Stockholm Declaration on Preventing Accidental Nuclear War is released.

December 4: The UN General Assembly adopts the Establishment of a Nuclear Weapons–Free Zone in the Middle East.

1991

July 31: Presidents Bush and Gorbachev sign the Strategic Arms Reduction Treaty (START).

1992

October 1: The United States initiates a nine-month moratorium on all nuclear weapons testing.

1993

SANE merges with several other pro-freeze organizations to become Peace Action.

January 3: START II is signed by the United States and Russia to reduce the nuclear arsenals of both nations to three thousand to thirty-five hundred long-range weapons and to eliminate all land-based missiles with MIRVs by 2003.

February 2: Due to radiation poisoning and pressure from the Nevada-Semipalatinsk Movement, Kazakhstan closes the Semipalatinsk nuclear weapons test site.

July 3: President Bill Clinton announces that he will extend the U.S. moratorium on nuclear weapons testing.

December 7: The U.S. Department of Energy reveals that the United States conducted 204 secret underground nuclear weapons tests over a forty-five-year period, deliberately exposing some Americans to dangerous levels of radiation without their consent.

December 8: The U.S. Air Force blows up an underground missile silo at Whitman Air Force Base in Missouri, the first of five hundred silos to be destroyed under the terms of START.

1994

January 14: Presidents Clinton and Boris Yeltsin announce that by the end of May no country will be targeted by either U.S. or Russian missiles.

March 14: President Clinton extends the moratorium on nuclear weapons testing through September 1995.

1995

February 25: Pope John Paul II calls for the abolition of all nuclear weapons.

April 25: Citizen organizations working toward nuclear weapons abolition adopt the Abolition 2000 Statement as the basis for a global effort to abolish nuclear weapons from the planet.

May 11: Signers of the NPT agree to extend the treaty indefinitely.

1996

March 25: The United States, France, and the United Kingdom sign three protocols to the Treaty of Rarotonga, which established a nuclear weapons–free zone in the South Pacific in 1985.

April 20: At the Nuclear Safety Summit in Moscow, the United States, Canada, France, Germany, the United Kingdom, Italy, Japan, and Russia affirm their commitment to sign the CTBT by September.

September 10: The UN General Assembly adopts the CTBT by a vote of 158 to 3 (Bhutan, India, and Libya) with five abstentions (Cuba, Lebanon, Mauritius, Syria, and Tanzania).

September 26: The United States, Russia, and Norway sign the Arctic Military and Environmental Cooperation Declaration to clean up nuclear waste dumped in the Arctic by the former Soviet military and to prevent future pollution.

1997

April: The Abolition 2000 Global Network releases a draft for a Nuclear Weapons Convention.

July 2: The United States breaks a five-year moratorium on nuclear weapons testing by conducting an underground test at the Nevada Test Site.

September 26: The United States and Russia agree to change the date for completing START II nuclear weapons reductions from January 1, 2003, to December 31, 2007, and to modify the 1972 ABM Treaty.

November: Developed in secret without Congressional or public input, Presidential Decision Directive 60, which asserts that the U.S. military will no longer attempt to win a nuclear war, is signed by President Clinton.

1998

April: The Pentagon issues a classified report for reducing the U.S. nuclear arsenal to under six thousand warheads, which is in accordance with START I.

1999

April 1: The U.S. Arms Control and Disarmament Agency merges into the State Department.

October 18: The U.S. Senate rejects ratification of the CTBT.

November 10: Russia threatens to abandon disarmament talks if the United States fails to adhere to the 1972 ABM Treaty.

2000

January 21: U.S. and Russian officials end nuclear disarmament talks in Geneva with no new agreements.

January 29: A Department of Energy study reveals a higher-than-normal frequency of cancer among six hundred thousand workers at fourteen nuclear power plants.

April 12: U.S. Energy Secretary Bill Richardson announces plans to compensate workers who became ill from radiation exposure in ten nuclear power plants during the so-called Cold War.

April 26: President Clinton vetoes the Nuclear Waste Policy Act calling for the storage of forty thousand tons of radioactive waste from U.S. nuclear power plants at Yucca Mountain in Nevada.

May 3: Civilian antinuclear organizations are permitted to make presentations at the NPT Review Conference at the United Nations.

June 6: Presidents Clinton and Vladimir Putin reach an Early Warning Agreement to reduce the risk of an accidental missile launch and to help prevent misinterpretations of events.

September 1: President Clinton announces the deferral of the national missile defense system (NMD); the United States and Russia enter into an agreement for each nation to begin disposing of thirty-four tons of weapons-grade plutonium, enough to make thousands of nuclear weapons.

October 19: Russia repeats its proposal for deep cuts in both the U.S. and Russian nuclear arsenals to fifteen hundred nuclear warheads or less under a START III treaty. However, Russia warns that the proposal depends on whether or not the U.S. undermines the 1972 ABM Treaty by developing the NMD system.

November 17–20: A Global Citizens' Assembly for the Elimination of Nuclear Weapons is held in Nagasaki, Japan, the last major antinuclear conference of the twentieth century.

December 14: Greenpeace calls on all NATO countries to oppose the U.S. NMD system. By forming a human chain across the main entrance to the NATO headquarters, they organize an international protest while foreign ministers meet to review arms control and disarmament policy.

December 14: The U.S. conducts its fifth nuclear weapons test this year in Nevada, inciting antinuclear activists who believe that these tests violate the CTBT.

2001

May 8: David Lochbaum, the nuclear safety engineer for the Union of Concerned Scientists, presents testimony to the U.S. Senate that exposes the laxity of the Nuclear Regulatory Commission (NRC) in enforcing updates and repairs to aging plants, publication of plant-specific risk studies, and improvements to plant security forces.

May 17: President George W. Bush revives the plan to pursue a permanent nuclear waste repository at Yucca Mountain in Nevada.

October 5: A Project on Government Oversight report exposes the vulnerability of ten U.S. nuclear weapons research and production facilities to terrorist attacks.

November 13: Presidents Bush and Putin pledge to reduce the U.S. nuclear arsenal to between seventeen hundred and twenty-two hundred weapons over the next ten years.

December 13: President Bush officially informs Russia of the U.S. withdrawal from the 1972 ABM Treaty and proceeds with plans to develop the NMD system.

2002
February 27: The Board of Directors of the *Bulletin of the Atomic Scientists* moves the minute hand of the "Doomsday Clock," the infamous symbol of nuclear danger, from nine to seven minutes to midnight, the same setting at which the clock debuted fifty-five years ago.

FOR FURTHER RESEARCH

Books

Robert C. Batchelder, *The Irreversible Decision: 1939–1950*. New York: Macmillan, 1961.

John W. Gofman and Arthur R. Tamplin, *Poisoned Power: The Case Against Nuclear Power Plants*. Emmaus, PA: Rodale, 1971.

Stephen Hilgartner, Richard C. Bell, and Rory O'Connor, *Nukespeak*. San Francisco: Sierra Club, 1982.

Robert D. Holsworth, *Let Your Life Speak: A Study of Politics, Religion, and Antinuclear Weapons Activism*. Madison: University of Wisconsin Press, 1989.

Carla B. Johnston, *Reversing the Nuclear Arms Race*. Cambridge, MA: Schenkman, 1986.

Christopher A. Kojm, ed., *The Nuclear Freeze Debate*. New York: Wilson, 1983.

Ernest W. Lefever and E. Stephen Hunt, eds., *The Apocalyptic Premise*. Washington, DC: Ethics and Public Policy Center, 1982.

Paul Rogat Loeb, *Hope in Hard Times: America's Peace Movement and the Reagan Era*. Lexington, KY: Lexington, 1987.

Katrina R. Mason, *The Children of Los Alamos: An Oral History of the Town Where the Atomic Age Began*. New York: Twayne, 1995.

Jerome Price, *The Antinuclear Movement*. Boston: Hall, 1990.

Richard Rashke, *The Killing of Karen Silkwood*. Ithaca, NY: Cornell University Press, 2000.

David Robie, *Eyes of Fire: The Last Voyage of the Rainbow Warrior*. Philadelphia: New Society, 1986.

Dorothy Rowe, *Living with the Bomb*. London: Routledge, 1985.

Jonathan Schell, *The Fate of the Earth*. New York: Knopf, 1982.

David N. Schwartz, *NATO's Nuclear Dilemmas*. Washington, DC: Brookings Institution, 1983.

William Sweet, *The Nuclear Age: Power, Proliferation, and the Arms Race*. Washington, DC: Congressional Quarterly, 1984.

Douglas C. Waller, *Congress and the Nuclear Freeze: An Inside Look at the Politics of a Mass Movement*. Amherst: University of Massachusetts Press, 1987.

Lawrence S. Wittner, *One World or None: A History of the World Nuclear Disarmament Movement Through 1953*. Vol. 1. CA: Stanford University Press, 1993.

————, *One World or None: A History of the World Nuclear Disarmament Movement, 1954–1970*. Vol. 2. CA: Stanford University Press, 1998.

Films

The China Syndrome. Dir. James Bridges. Columbia/Tristar, 1979.

The Day After. Dir. Nicholas Meyer. Anchor Bay Entertainment, 1983.

Silkwood. Dir. Mike Nichols. Anchor Bay Entertainment, 1983.

War Games. Dir. John Badham. MGM/UA, 1983.

Internet Sources

Russell Bertrand and Albert Einstein, "The Russell-Einstein Manifesto," July 9, 1955. www.nuclearfiles.org.

Dorothy Day, "We Go on Record: The CW Response to Hiroshima," *Catholic Worker*, September 1945. www.catholicworker.org.

James Franck et al., *Report of the Committee on Political and Social Problems (The Franck Report)*, June 1945. Ed. Gene Dannen. www.dannen.com.

Daryl G. Kimball, "Ending Nuclear Terror," *National Debate*, Winter 1998. www.clw.org.

David Krieger, "U.S. Nuclear Weapons Policy After September 11th," January 14, 2002. www.wagingpeace.org.

John M. LaForge, "Hiroshima's and Nagasaki's Lessons Still to Be Learned," *Z Magazine*, July/August 1998. http://zena. secureforum.com.

David Lochbaum, "Safety of Old and New Reactors," *Union of Concerned Scientists' Testimony to the U.S. Senate Subcommittee on Clean Air, Wetlands, Private Property, and Nuclear Safety*, May 8, 2001. www.ucsusa.org.

Leo Maley III and Uday Mohan, "Second-Guessing Hiroshima," *History News Service*, July 29, 1998. www2.h-net.msu. edu.

Nuclear Age Peace Foundation, "Six Arguments for Abolishing Nuclear Weapons," 1998. www.abolition2000.org.

Dorothy Purley, "Uranium Mining and the Laguna People," *Synthesis/Regeneration*, Spring 1996. www.greens.org.

John A. Simpson, "A Challenge for the 21st Century," *Bulletin of the Atomic Scientists*, November/December 1995. www. thebulletin.org.

Grace Thorpe, "Our Homes Are Not Dumps: Creating Nuclear-Free Zones," North American Native Workshop on Environmental Justice, Iliff School of Theology, Denver. www.alphacdc.com/necona/homes, March 17, 1995.

Kinue Tomoyasu, "Testimony of Kinue Tomoyasu," *The Voice of Hibakusha*, September 29, 1999. www.inicom.com.

Periodicals

David Cortright, "Ban the Bomb II: A New Movement Emerges to Abolish Nuclear Weapons," *Sojourners*, January/February 1999.

John Hershey, "Hiroshima," *New Yorker*, August 31, 1946.

Daniel Hirsch, "The NRC: What, Me Worry?" *Bulletin of the Atomic Scientists*, January/February 2002.

Chris Knap, "Recent Safety Hazards at Aging Nuclear Power Plants," *Orange County Register*, December 9, 2001.

Brook Larmer, "Chernobyl Disaster Reawakens Anti-Nuclear Movement in US," *Christian Science Monitor*, May 27, 1986.

Roger C. Molander, "How I Learned to Start Worrying and Hate the Bomb," *Washington Post*, March 21, 1982.

Jonathan Schell, "The New Nuclear Danger," *Nation*, June 25, 2001.

Lynn Smith, "She Crusades for Nuclear 'Downwinders'" *Los Angeles Times*, March 6, 1987.

Mark Sommer, "Cutting 'Nukes' Stockpiles," *Christian Science Monitor*, November 17, 1992.

Raymond Swing, "Albert Einstein on the Atomic Bomb," *Atlantic Monthly*, November 1945.

W.K. Wyant Jr., "50,000 Baby Teeth," *Nation*, June 13, 1959.

Websites

Abolition 2000, www.abolition2000.org. A global network of antinuclear organizations calling for the abolition of the world's nuclear arsenals.

American Friends Service Committee, www.afsc.org. AFSC is a Quaker organization that includes people of various faiths who are committed to social justice, peace, and humanitarian service.

Atomic Archive, www.atomicarchive.com. This site explores the history surrounding the invention of the atomic bomb.

Atomic Bomb: Decision, www.dannen.com. This site houses documents, reproduced in text form, concerning the decision to use the atomic bomb.

Bulletin of the Atomic Scientists, www.bullatomsci.org. Founded in 1945 by several disillusioned Manhattan Project scientists, the *Bulletin* continues to educate citizens about the dangers posed by nuclear and other weapons of mass destruction and the appropriate roles of nuclear technology.

Campaign for Nuclear Disarmament, www.cnduk.org. CND's tactics include direct action, protests, lobbying, letter writing, and speaking in schools and public meetings.

Chernobyl Poems of Lyubov Sirota, www.wsu.edu. This site showcases the work of a woman who witnessed the explosion at the Chernobyl Atomic Energy Station in 1986. She continues to suffer from radiation exposure, having contracted cataracts as well as a brain tumor.

Coalition to Reduce Nuclear Dangers, www.crnd.org. Currently the largest alliance of international arms control and disarmament groups.

Committee on Disarmament, www.peacenet.org. The committee has provided services and facilities to hundreds of citizens' groups concerned with nuclear disarmament.

Council for a Livable World, www.clw.org. Among the nation's leading arms control organizations, CLW focuses on halting the spread of weapons of mass destruction and opposing a national missile defense system.

Downwinders, www.downwinders.org. Founded in 1978, this research and educational foundation works to expose the plight of residents who live or have lived downwind of the Nevada test site and have developed cancers and other illnesses from fallout radiation. The foundation also works to obtain compensation for all Downwinders and to end all nuclear testing at the Nevada test site and elsewhere.

Fellowship of Reconciliation, www.forusa.org. The largest and oldest interfaith peace organization in the United States.

Green Parties World Wide, www.greens.org. An international organization that focuses on ecological wisdom, grassroots democracy, social justice, and peace and nonviolence.

Hiroshima Peace Cultural Center, www.inicom.com. This site provides survivors' accounts of the bombing of Hiroshima.

Leo Szilard Online, www.dannen.com. An electronic archive of the work and life of Leo Szilard, the loudest voice of dissension among the concerned Manhattan Project scientists.

National Environmental Coalition of Native Americans, www.alphacdc.com. This group works to keep nuclear waste off Indian lands.

Nuclear Abolition Project, www.gracelinks.org. In collaboration with Abolition 2000, this project works to abolish global nuclear arsenals and find new solutions for the health and environmental consequences of nuclear waste.

Nuclear Age Peace Foundation, www.wagingpeace.org. The foundation focuses on initiatives to eliminate nuclear weapons and achieve peace through education and advocacy.

Nuclear Files, www.nuclearfiles.org. A project of the Nuclear Age Peace Foundation, this site provides extensive background information, as well as primary and secondary documents, on nuclear weapons and nuclear war.

Nukewatch: People Working for an End to Nuclear Power and Weapons, www.nukewatch.com. Nukewatch is a Wisconsin-based environmental and peace action group dedicated to the abolition of nuclear weapons and nuclear power.

Peace Action, www.peace-action.org. The National Committee for a Sane Nuclear Policy (SANE) officially merged with other activist organizations in 1987, undergoing a name change in 1993 to Peace Action. Currently the largest grassroots organization in the United States, Peace Action works to achieve the abolition of nuclear weapons and promotes nonmilitary solutions to international conflicts.

Physicians for Social Responsibility, www.psr.org. PSR works to reduce and eliminate nuclear weapons, wisely dispose of nuclear material from retired weapons, and clean up contaminated nuclear facilities.

Project Abolition, www.projectabolition.org. Founded in 1999 as an umbrella organization for antinuclear grassroots groups, this project focuses on increasing public awareness of nuclear dangers and achieving the abolition of global nuclear arsenals.

Project Whistlestop, www.trumanlibrary.org. This site offers primary documents related to the decision to develop and use the atomic bomb.

Proposition One Committee, http://prop1.org. Proposition One is a grassroots movement concerned with nuclear disarmament and the conversion of nuclear and other arms industries to provide for human and environmental needs.

Union of Concerned Scientists, www.ucsusa.org. Founded in 1969, the UCS works to reduce the risks from nuclear power, promote alternatives to nuclear energy, and rid the world of nuclear weapons.

Women's Action for New Directions, www.wand.org. Founded as Women's Action for Nuclear Disarmament by Dr. Helen Caldicott in the early 1980s to end the threat of nuclear annihilation, WAND continues to empower women to act politically, to reduce militarism and violence, and to redirect excessive military resources toward human and environmental needs.

Women's International League for Peace and Freedom, www.
wilpf.int.ch. Founded in 1915, this organization works to
organize women of different political and philosophical
convictions in order to abolish the political, social, economic, and psychological causes of war and work for a
constructive peace.

nuclear weapons
admitting uselessness of, 81–83
costs, 73–74, 152
Cuban missile crisis and, 53
disclosing secret military programs
on, 79–80
elimination of, 152–53
addressing obstacles and problems
with, 89–90
new movement for, 160–64
vs. pursuing missile defense
system, 157–58
rogue states and, 90–91
steps to, 87–89, 154–57
U.S. pledge to, 87, 92–94
verification measures for, 152–53
as encouraging vs. deterring war,
150
have not prevented wars, 72–73
illegal use or threat of, 71
international agreement on
prevention of, 37–38
as morally reprehensible, 72
mutual assured destruction through.
See mutual assured destruction
new threat and roles of, 20–21,
159–60, 167–69, 173
as posing risks for U.S. security,
85–86
remembering humanity vs., 43
terrorist threat cannot be deterred
with, 151
U.S. arsenal, 160
used against non-nuclear states,
78–79
see also nuclear policy
nuclear weapons freeze
arms race and, 64, 66–67
vs. a global freeze, 69
Kennedy-Hatfield resolution on, 19
leading to mutual reductions, 64–65
Reagan administration and, 63
scientific community's demand for,
42–43
START proposal and, 63–64
verifying adherence to, 68–69
nuclear weapons free zones, 157
Nukespeak, 16
Nunn, Sam, 148, 154, 175
Nunn-Lugar Program, 147–48, 156,
175, 178

O'Connor, Rory, 16
O'Leary, Hazel, 79
Operational Safeguards Response
Evaluation (OSRE) program,
140–41
Oppenheimer, J. Robert, 12
Oyster Creek plant (New Jersey),
120, 122

Pacific Gas & Electric (PG&E),
136–37
pacifism. *See* religious pacifists
Paguate, New Mexico, 191–95
Pakistan, 73, 168, 177
Palmetto Alliance, 105
Pax Christi USA, 162
Peace Action, 19, 21
Peacemaker, The (movie), 146
pebble-bed reactor design, 128–29,
144
Pentagon budget, 80
People's Power Project, 17
Perry, William, 76
Persian Gulf bombing campaign, 76
Physicians for Social Responsibility,
18, 21
plutonium, 101, 116–17
Pojoaque Pueblo (New Mexico), 111
Pollard, Robert, 119
Potomac Alliance, 104
Prairie Island, Minnesota, 110
Prairie Island Sioux, 112
Price, Jerome, 96
Project Abolition, 19, 21, 166
Project ELF, 80
protests. *See* demonstrations
Public Media Center of California,
101
Pugwash Conference on Science and
World Affairs, 14
Purley, Dorothy, 191
Putin, Vladimir V., 163

Quakers, 24

Rabinowitch, Eugene, 11–12
radiation
from uranium mines, 109–10

Radioactive Waste Management Act, 110

radioactive wastes
antinuclear movement activism and, 106
secrecy of, 80

Ramberg, Bennett, 134

reactor waste disposal. *See* nuclear waste disposal

Reagan administration
antinuclear movement during, 106–107
nuclear weapons freeze and, 63
proposals to, 67–68

religious pacifists, 13
advocating personal and communal resistance to arms race, 27
on atomic weaponry, 25–26
evangelism and, 27–28
history of activism by, 24–25
"personalist orientation" of, 26–27
Vatican II and, 28–30
World War II, 25

renewable energy, 20

Report of the Manhattan Project Met Lab Committee on Political and Social Problems, 11–12

Rerum Novarum (Leo XIII), 28

Rickover, Hyman G., 66

rogue states
elimination of nuclear weapons and, 90–91
military budget, 78
new role of nuclear weapons and, 160

Roosevelt, Franklin D., 11

Rosenbaum report, 97

Rotblat, Joseph, 72, 84

Russell, Bertrand, 14, 16, 39

Russell-Einstein Manifesto, 14–15

Russia
Berlin crisis and, 53–55
nuclear arsenals of, 167
nuclear capability, 64
on prospect of nuclear warfare, 34–35
responding to false nuclear missile attack, 148–49
scientific discovery in, 33
stolen nuclear materials from, 146–47
U.S. funding for securing nuclear arsenals in, 147–48, 156, 175, 178

Safe Energy Coalition, 99

Safe Power in Maine, 100

SALT (Strategic Arms Limitation Talks), 16

SALT II Treaty, 67–68

SANE. *See* National Committee for a Sane Nuclear Policy

San Onofre Unit (California), 122

Saudi Arabia, 99

Schell, Jonathan, 21–22, 165, 196

Schmidt, Helmut, 83

Schweitzer, Albert, 15

scientific community
American vs. European discoveries, 32–33
antinuclear sentiments in, 13–14
on arguments for test detonations in Japan, 36–37
conference for, 14–15
educating public and policy makers, 20–21
government ignoring opinion of, 11
on international agreement for prevention of nuclear arms, 37–38
on potential destruction of nuclear war, 40–42
on safety of arms race, 33–34
unite to avoid a nuclear holocaust, 41

Seabrook nuclear power plant, 103

Second Vatican Council, 28–30

secret military programs, 79–80

September 11, 2001
Bush's response to, 174–75
as demonstrating inadequacy of security rules, 135–36
as having little impact on nuclear policy, 177–78
Nuclear Regulatory Commission response to, 134, 142–43
possible nuclear policy in response to, 175–77
questions raised by, 131–32

shelter programs, 58–59

Sierra Club, 100, 102

Silkwood, Karen, 17, 97–98, 100, 101,